THE PRESIDENTIAL NOMINATING PROCESS

The George Gund Lectures
Volume I

Edited by

Kenneth W. Thompson
Director
The White Burkett Miller Center of Public Affairs
University of Virginia

UNIVERSITY
PRESS OF
AMERICA

LANHAM • NEW YORK • LONDON

Copyright © 1983 by

University Press of America,™ Inc.

4720 Boston Way
Lanham, MD 20706

3 Henrietta Street
London WC2E 8LU England

Library of Congress Cataloging in Publication Data
Main entry under title:

The Presidential nominating process.

　　Lectures organized by the White Burkett Miller
Center of Public Affairs.
　　1. Presidents—United States—Nomination—Addresses,
essays, lectures. I. Thompson, Kenneth W., 1921-
II. White Burkett Miller Center.
JK521.P733　1983　　　324.5'0973　　　83-6790
ISBN 0-8191-3256-X (v. 1)
ISBN 0-8191-3257-8 (pbk. : v. 1)

Dedicated
to
all those who search
for
better American Presidents
and to two
Special Friends
of
the Miller Center
Melvin Laird
and
James Lipscomb

TABLE OF CONTENTS

PREFACE

In the past two years, the Miller Center has organized two major national commissions, the first concerned with presidential press conferences and the second with the presidential nominating process. Surrounding both these efforts, the Center has brought together scholars, journalists and public figures to illuminate the problems. Joining with members of the staff, these authorities have provided resource material for the two commissions. They have also written scholarly papers and delivered lectures in the Dome Room of the Rotunda. These lectures and papers constitute an invaluable body of thought and knowledge supplementing the two commission reports.

The leadership of the Miller Center and its governing Council have determined to make available these papers and lectures hoping thereby to stimulate greater public interest in the subject. We are profoundly indebted to the George Gund Foundation of Cleveland for its generous assistance in making possible the lectures on the nominating process and the Miller Center Commission on the Presidential Nominating Process. We also wish to thank the Reader's Digest Foundation and the Mobil Foundation for lending their support to the work of the commission as well.

INTRODUCTION

The aim of the Center in the organization of the George Gund Lecture Series has been to bring to the University of Virginia the most original and challenging thinkers on the presidential nominating process. We have sought diversity of approaches, not representatives of a single viewpoint. Wherever possible, we have tried to balance conflicting philosophies of political science and political theory. Thus one of the contributors is an authority on American political parties and presidential selection who is also thoroughly grounded in classical political theory. Another presidential scholar who took part in the series has been in the forefront of those who have promoted political behaviorism. A third is a prominent writer and public servant who organized and edited a series of round-robin papers sent out by the Aspen Institute.

The common characteristic of all the lecturers is the clarity and forcefulness of their views. James W. Ceaser is a brilliant young political theorist and student of American government at the University of Virginia who was the author of the draft report of the Miller Center Commission on the Presidential Nominating Process. The breadth of his thought and his intellectual versatility is reflected in the first chapter in the volume. Douglass Cater is the newly appointed president of Washington College who for three decades has written essays on politics and public affairs in popular and scholarly journals. In his paper, he examines the views of the founders and the prevailing constitutional perspectives on presidential selection. Cater brings the story up to date by comparing the political problems and circumstances at the time of the founders with those existing at the present time.

Part Two shifts attention from the history and theory of the nominating process to the political process and the role of political parties. Senator Eugene McCarthy discussed "The President, the Public and the Nominating Process" ranging

1

across a broad spectrum of cultural, social and political factors that influence presidential selection. In his approach, he considers the role of money and television in more outspoken terms than any of the other speakers. Professor Tom Cronin is a professor of political science at Colorado College who has collaborated with his colleague, Bob Loevy, in the writing of a paper on the role of political parties in presidential nominations. His reformist views are more far-reaching than those of any other contributor.

Austin Ranney, past president of the American Political Science Association and research scholar at the American Enterprise Institute, concludes the discussion in Part Three with an analysis of candidates, coalitions, institutions and reforms.

PART ONE

THE THEORY and HISTORY
of
PRESIDENTIAL SELECTION

THE THEORY of the PRESIDENTIAL NOMINATING PROCESS

James W. Ceaser

MR. THOMPSON: We are pleased to welcome you to a George Gund lecture on the presidential nominating process. Today it seems appropriate that the author of the Miller Center commission report on the presidential nominating process, Professor James Ceaser, should be the speaker.

Yesterday I made a hurried trip to New York to meet with a group of a dozen or so distinguished Americans. They included former cabinet members like Bill Simon and Cyrus Vance; White House aides like Lloyd Cutler; a former Attorney General, Herbert Brownell; current cabinet members like Malcolm Baldridge and others. We met to talk about the whole issue of the choice and the nomination of a President and the term of office which such a President should serve. I was struck by the fact that the two issues that seemed to be most prevalent in their discussion were, first, the issue of picking the ablest possible candidate through the political process, and secondly, providing that candidate, however able or however limited from whatever human standpoint, with the means and the tools of governing. As I thought about that discussion and thought back to the first publication of Professor Ceaser, his book *Presidential Selection: Theory and Development*, and the criteria he established, I was struck by the fact that everything that the group said yesterday in one way or another seemed to relate to the five criteria that Professor Ceaser formulated in his first and very important book. He states in that book that the five functions of a presidential selection system should be to minimize the harmful effects of ambitious contenders for office, to promote responsible executive leadership and power, to

5

help secure an able President, to insure a legitimate succession, and to provide for an appropriate amount of choice and change.

That study and his subsequent *Reforming the Reforms* book for the Twentieth Century Fund represent a concerted effort by a younger scholar. In a day and age when it is sometimes said that the system operates against younger scholars, Professor Ceaser proves that axiom wrong. In the first place, Professor Ceaser fairly early in his career established himself as an extraordinarily popular teacher of American government. Next, very quickly through his publications and lectures, he gained the recognition necessary for a tenured appointment in the department. Now all of us watch with wary eyes as the nation itself has discovered what Virginia had discovered, that a quite exceptional younger scholar is a member of the government department at the University of Virginia.

We have felt unusually privileged, then, that as we undertook the nominating commission study with a very distinguished membership and chaired by Adlai Stevenson III and Melvin Laird, that Professor Ceaser has provided the analytic competence necessary for such a study and made possible the marriage which inevitably has to take place between any national commission, however distinguished, and those who bring to bear on the discussion the resources of scholarship, knowledge and understanding. If the commission's report has any impact (and as late as ten thirty this morning a radio station in Dallas evidently thought it had considerable impact because they devoted half an hour of discussion to the commission's report) the major credit must go to Professor Ceaser.

So without any further extension of my remarks, I want to let all of you know that the core effort in the work of the Miller Center commission—to bring together the thoughts of a large number of people and a considerable number of writers on the subject of the nominating process—was carried out by our speaker.

PROFESSOR CEASER: Thank you, Professor Thompson, for your very kind introduction and for the efforts that you, the Gund Foundation, and the Miller Center have made to bring greater public awareness about the presidential nominating process.

Like the other speakers in this series, I feel a deep sense of awe in being asked to speak in this, the most majestic room of Thomas Jefferson's magnificent architectural design for the University of Virginia. So it is fitting, I think, that I should begin with a statement of Thomas Jefferson.

Writing to a friend in 1789, Jefferson said, "If I could not go to heaven but with a political party, I would not go there at all." What an amazing degree of self confidence Jefferson must have had to impose conditions on his entrance into heaven. We must suppose, therefore, that at this point in his life he had a profound dislike for political parties. And yet we know that Jefferson became the first national partisan leader in American history, helping to found and sustain what are the rudiments of today's Democratic party, the oldest mass-based political party in the world. And we know also that Jefferson, despite his earlier animus against political parties, seemed in the dusk of his life to have reconciled himself to their existence and even accorded them faint praise. In 1822 he wrote, "I consider that party division of Whig and Tory," by which he meant Federalist and Republican, "the most wholesome which can exist in any government and well worthy of being nourished to keep out those of the more dangerous character." Jefferson, then, was ambivalent in his attitude towards parties. And this must lead us to wonder whether, when he entered heaven, as we must surely suppose he did, he took his political party with him.

Jefferson's ambivalence about the best means of one man's personal salvation is representative of our entire nation's attitude towards political parties, which also has been one of ambivalence. It has ranged—from an Olympian distaste on the part of the Founding Fathers, to a warm enthusiasm on the part of many recent reformers. We must begin today, therefore, with the same question that perplexed Mr. Jefferson: What is the path to political salvation? Does it lie with or without political parties or, modifying those questions to fit present circumstances, is it to be found with or without political parties that are strong and effective?

The question is properly posed at this moment. We have just passed through an extraordinary period of reform. It began in 1968 at the Democratic National Convention in Chicago when New Politics advocates and anti-war activists forced the issue of reform on the Democratic party. Subsequently, the movement for reform reached out to touch every major

7

national institution, with the possible exception of the Supreme Court. Parties, Congress, the Presidency, and the electoral process were all influenced in one way or another by the tide of reform. In fact, in a book which I will have occasion to discuss later on, Samuel Huntington's *American Politics: The Promise of Democracy,* the reform period of the late 1960's and early '70's is ranked along with three other major reform periods in American History: the Revolutionary War, the Jacksonian era, and the progressive era. In this view, at least, the institutional changes of the last decade were among the most profound that we have experienced in our entire history.

Yet it now seems clear that the reform impulse of the last decade has lost its force and vigor. It is not just that the radicals of the 1960's now find themselves in the awkward position of meeting mortgage payments. It is that political leaders of all persuasions have begun to feel that the government does not operate effectively under the conditions created by the recent reforms. But one cannot assume that a mere feeling of disappointment over the reforms will produce the necessary impetus for change. Today the impulse for reform has weakened, but the question remains: What is to be done? One can sit still and accommodate oneself to the changes of the last decade, or one can think about developing a new agenda for reforming the reforms.

To decide what to do, it is necessary to look first at the underpinnings of the reform movement. Reform was offered as a general doctrine for governing and as a means of political salvation. We can ask, therefore, what were the sacred commandments of this movement. I could have cited ten, but following the recent example of the *Reader's Digest Bible,* I have taken the liberty of abbreviating the decalogue. Here, then, are the five commandments of reform: First, thou shalt not use the people's name in vain. Put differently, the reform movement supported a populist notion of government, endorsing the adage that "The cure for the evils of democracy is more democracy."

Second, thou shalt not make unto thyself any graven image—that is, no donkeys and no elephants. Put differently, the reform movement sought to reduce the discretion of representative institutions, in particular that of our political parties.

Third, thou shalt keep the election day holy. Put differently, the reform movement displayed a profound concern for democratic procedures and was especially intent on increasing the number of primary elections. Little attention, however, was paid to the efforts of such changes on the activity of governing.

Fourth, thou shalt not steal, corrupt, give the appearance of corruption, spend too much money on campaigns, or outspend thy opponent. Put differently, the reform movement devised some of the most complicated legislation ever written in an effort to end corruption in campaigns, reduce the influence of "big money" and interest groups, equalize campaign expenditures, and reduce the amount of money spent on campaigns. Fifth, Thou shalt not lie. Put differently, the reform movement sought not only honesty in government, but an extraordinary degree of openness. Except for the term "the people," the words "open" and "openness" were among the most frequently employed in the political rhetoric of the last decade. This sentiment led to open committee hearings, sunshine laws, sunset legislation, the legal obligation on the part of politicians to reveal their financial records, and details of their personal lives.

These are the five commandments of the sacred tablet of reform. But are they the rules that can lead us to political salvation? Or are they a golden calf that will lead us down the path of error? Today, more and more people are dissatisfied with at least some of the reforms. But few are prepared to admit that they actually represent Aaron's golden calf. No, the chief explanation, including the apologia of many who have recanted from reform thought, is not exactly that a sin of commission was committed, but rather than reformers could not find the path to salvation. The reform canons were intended, it was said, in the right spirit. Somehow or other, however, the consequences turned out differently than expected. It was ignorance, not willful malice, that was the cause of the failures of reform.

I will not bother to elaborate on all the unintended consequences of reform, since they have been so ably discussed in the chapters which follow. Let it suffice to give a quick survey. In regard to popular control of the presidential nominating process, the reforms have succeeded in giving us a set of rules that *looks* more democratic. But perceptions can be illusory. Voter turnout in primaries has been disappointingly low and has been skewed in such a way that it tends to "underrepresent" the poorer and less well-educated segments of the electorate. Moreover, because our primary elections for presidential nominees are scheduled over a long sequence, it often turns out that by the time many voters have the chance to vote, the nominating decision has already been made. It is a strange exercise of democracy to ask citizens to vote when the results are already known! Finally, the sequence of primary elections has worked in such a way as to give an extraordinary degree of influence to the media. Public opinion at each step in the process is in part formed by the media's presentation of the results of the preceeding step. The media do indeed present the news, but the news itself is a presentation of information that tends to emphasize the new (a "new face" is emerging on the American presidential scene), to play up the deviation of an event from expectations (a certain candidate may have lost a primary but did "better than expected" and is therefore "coming on"), and to give more weight than reality itself to making political events into archetypal stories (such as the story of David, the political "outsider" with no organization, slaying Goliath, the big front-runner with lots of cash in his campaign war chests).

In regard to the reformers' efforts to eliminate the influence of "special interests," they did in fact succeed in reducing the power of certain corrupt party machines and of eliminating individual "fat cat" contributors. Yet these gains have come at quite a price. The declining power of parties has given more, not less, influence to single interest groups in society, which now can press their views more easily on unshielded candidates. The influence, for example, of the NEA on certain candidates in 1980 was notorious. As in campaign financing, the elimination of the individual "fat cat" has given way, at least in congressional elections, to an extraordinary influence by well-organized professional fund-raising organizations—the political action committees. These groups operate without any of the sentimentality of certain fat cats and look for a solid return on their investments.

As much as I agree, then, that there are all these unanticipated consequences of reform, and that these consequences were, for the most part, worse than the intentions, I do not think that the matter can or should be left at that. The problem with the reform movement lies not simply with the consequences that went astray, but with an understanding of democracy and of our political process that was partial and ill-conceived. Let us, for a moment, attempt to reconstruct the theory of government that underlies the reform impulse. It can be taken from some of the commandments that I discussed.

First, we can mention the theme of populism. If anyone were to look at the political rhetoric of our presidential candidates in the years from 1968 to 1976, they would discover an extraordinary degree of populism even by American standards. By populism I mean style of leadership in which a leader asserts a position not with the understanding that it is a standard to which people are to rally, but rather with the understanding that it expresses what the people *already* want. If you look at political dialogue of the 1970's you find leaders unwilling to assert a position without simultaneously claiming that it represented the will of the people. By 1976, our leaders had gone further. It was not the positions they asserted which were said to represent the people's will, but rather something, so to speak, beneath these positions. Candidate Jimmy Carter ran a campaign that was based principally on being able to articulate the people's wants, hopes, and fears. We moved from issue populism to thematic populism. The notion of leadership seemed to be that of who best could immerse his will into that of the people.

The next theme of reform was popular participation. At the same time that the rhetoric of our presidential campaigns was filled with populist sentiments, more and more people began to speak of the need for participation, for direct action by the public in all fundamental decisionmaking processes. This tendency was most evident in the presidential selection process. Since the leader was thought to embody the sovereign will of the public, it followed that everyone must therefore have a say not only in his election, but in his nomination as well. Under the influence of this view, the prerogative of political party leaders to nominate presidential candidates was challenged and eventually taken away. The theme of participatory democracy was not limited, however, to a discussion of the problems in presidential nominations. Reformers called for a plan for direct election of the President, national registration by mail, and a constitutional amendment that would allow for national referendums. Reformers declared that such anticipatory initiatives would not only make national policymaking, more responsive to the will of the citizenry, but also that it would foster citizen virtue by opening up new opportunities for political participation.

The final theme of reform was openness. Even with leaders speaking for the people and even with so many decisions made directly by the people, some discretion, it turns out, of necessity has to be left with the decisionmakers. One way, however, that the public can "participate" without being able directly to make the decisions is if the decisionmaker's every action is fully open. The public can then step in and, in the case of error, make sure that the policy is changed. So government—in theory—is opened up. But it is not so much the people as the journalists who gain from this process of opening everything to public purview. The media arrogates to itself the special role of the watchdog or spokesmen for the public, pushing its prerogatives under the solemn banner of the "public's right to know."

I said that the theory on which the reform was based was partial and ill-conceived. In making the claim that it was partial, I mean to suggest that it does have a certain foundation in the American political tradition. After all, this is a nation which is governed by "the consent of the governed." And that great phrase, the consent of the governed, has given rise to two interpretations of the legitimate form of public rule in America. One is that strain which we can call democratic or populist. The other is one we can call representative or republican. The democratic impulse, in one form or another, pushes for popular control, participation, and the control of elites and hierarchies by the public. The other emphasizes insitutional forms, discretion for leadership, and statesmanship.

Both of these strains were present at the Founding and were represented in the parties that disputed over the Constitution, the Anti-Federalists and the Federalists. But it is interesting to observe that the democratic side, which was embodied in the Anti-Federalists position, had a strikingly different character than that espoused by the modern proponents of mass democracy. In the view of the Anti-Federalists, the positive benefits of democracy derived from the activity of governing in local governments. It was in local politics that the people could know the issues, and it was here, by means of a continual involvement in local life, that citizen virtue could be fostered. Citizens could identify their interests with the community and in so doing learn the arts of citizenship. At the national level, by contrast, the Anti-Federalists, while favoring somewhat more democratic government than the Federalists, did not expect any positive benefits. Democratic forms at the national level in their view, were justified chiefly as damage control devices. Power far away from home was dangerous, and democratic techniques could be used to prevent leaders, who were greatly mistrusted, from doing anything very much at all. The Anti-Federalists were jealous of national power, and they relied on democratic techniques to constrain and confine it. The weaker the national government, the safer were the liberties of the people.

The modern case for democracy is altogether different. It is based on democracy at the national level. Local politics and prerogatives have been disparaged, and the focus has been placed upon national politics. National politics and executive leadership are seen as the sources for positive action and for creative policymaking. Through populism, public control at the national level is embodied in a leader. Through the public's right to know and through popular participation, the people keep their government in check. No wonder with such an extraordinary amount of power granted and such jealousy towards it we have the condition of ungovernability.

The essence of the case for mass democracy is a belief that we can obtain the positive elements of the Anti-Federalists' position through national participation. But this is a certain prescription for failure. It cannot and it will not work. It gives the illusion of participation, but strips it of most of its content. The citizen virtue that is supposed to come through participation in politics cannot be the result of the meager act of voting in presidential primaries. There is an amazing disproportion between the means and the end, between the desire for citizen virtue and the activity of going to an election booth and pulling a lever. If citizen virtue is to mean anything, it must include an ongoing commitment of the citizen in politics in which the citizen can engage in contact and dialogue with other citizens. Nor is it reasonable to expect that most citizens can have the time or knowledge to make decisions on issues far away from the common sense judgement of ordinary people. And so here, too, there is an illusion or gap between the expectation of participation and its reality.

Where, then, does that leave the democratic impulse? Contrary to what the Anti-Federalists had thought, it has been found essential that many aspects of political power must be exercised on the national level. A weak and impotent federal government could suffice in the nineteenth century, but it certainly cannot suffice today. So this leaves us with a problem. The Anti-Federalist position would seem to have no recourse, save a futile and blind objection to the forces of modernity. But I believe this is not the case. In fact, the American political system has developed a kind of synthesis which is embodied in the institution of the political party. Built up from the contacts formed most often at the state and local levels, the political party is the instrument which bridges the Federalists and Anti-Federalist tradition. The political party does not hold out the illusory prospect that citizens can be virtuous through direct participation in national politics. But it does enable citizens in their localities to have some say in national politics in a setting in which citizens can meet with other citizens. Their political opinions emerge and are filtered up through the ranks. The party can serve as one vehicle where citizens learn about politics. The party can be one of Tocqueville's "schools of liberty." The political party does not normally preach a simple populism. But it does enable a greater number of citizens to have input into national politics. The political party curbs and moderates the Federalists' and the Constitution's distant notions of representation and statesmanship. But it does so without removing all or even most discretion on the part of governing officials.

Now, I have absolutely nothing against reform *per se*. But I do think that the proof should be in the pudding, and for that I wanted to turn a moment to a recent book published by a Harvard professor of government, Samuel Huntington. Huntington sees that there are certain key periods in American history which he calls periods of creedal passion, which serve, so to speak, as the great moments of conscience in American history. These periods are the revolutionary period, the Jacksonian period, the progressive period, and the period of the late sixties and early seventies. It is in these moments, argues Huntington, that the essential American creed, which he identifies as a democratic or participatory one, rises up against the forces of institutional resistance and presses upon the structures of government to open things up to change. The American creed in Huntington's view is the democratic impulse. It rears its head episodically when the processes of normal politics seem to frustrate the participation of the many.

This thesis of American politics is defective in two essential respects. In the first place, it identifies the American creed with what is in fact only one-half of the American tradition. It proclaims that the American principles are Anti-Federalist or democratic principles. But it wholly overlooks the Federalist or representative impulse. This interpretation, therefore, gives full legitimacy to the radical tradition in American politics while denying any legitimacy to its moderating tradition. Such an interpretation is not only incorrect, but unhelpful, even by Huntington's own standards. Huntington himself finds great wisdom in representative principles, but he is left in the uncomfortable and unnecessary position of maintaining that these have no standing in the American tradition.

In the second place, Huntington greatly exaggerates the importance of reform periods in relation to periods in which substantive changes in policies have been made. The "soul" of American political dialogue, in his view, concerns the struggle for direct democracy rather than the ends of rule. But the latter is as important—even more important—than the former. And the plain fact of the matter is that many of the great historical struggles have involved matters of substance without very much concern about whether our parties, Congress, or the presidency should be made more or less democratic.

Remarkably, what is omitted in Huntington's presentation are those moments when the people talked less about procedural reforms and yet nonetheless proceeded to the tasks of true reform. In this entire book there is only one reference to Abraham Lincoln. Franklin Delano Roosevelt and the New Deal period receive only scant attention. And despite its publication date, nothing was said about President Reagan. Yet it has been in these periods—1860, 1936, and perhaps 1980—that we have had important changes in the *substance* of our policies. These changes have come without any great procedural reforms, without any calls for direct democracy. And they have come by using the political party as the chief instrument for effectuating change.

With this in mind, then, I conclude that we should do everything we can to keep our parties strong and effective. That raises the question of what is to be done. Before suggesting a few concrete proposals, I would like to make a couple of preliminary comments about the process of institutional reform in the case of the presidential nominating process. In the first place, it should be evident from what I have said before that the question of change in the presidential selection process is part of a larger set of issues, of the condition of parties, of attitudes about representative government and popular rule. One could, of course, make isolated changes in the presidential selection process. And it may well be the case that it would be better to begin here because this is the most visible of all the activities of our political parties and the focal point today of so much concern. But in the final analysis significant change in the nominating process can only fully be realized in conjunction with other changes in the role of political parties and with changes in some common doctrine about the importance of political parties in our representative scheme of government.

In the second place, I would much prefer to see change come, not so much by way of a single general plan, as by way of an ongoing process. By a plan I mean one comprehensive set of proposals that one can lay out on the table and that would be implemented by a central authority, with all the expected consequences known in advance. That, I think, is not the best mode of proceeding. By a process, on the other hand, I mean a change in decision making authority in which, over the course of time, various changes would be made on an incremental basis tending towards a given aim or result.

With those two comments in mind, let me just suggest four or five concrete steps that could be taken. *First, denationalizing the rules of the Democratic party.* One of the reasons that we have had so many reforms in the selection of our presidential candidate has been the intrusion of national Democratic party rules into the laws and rules of state parties with respect to the selection of delegates. I would start by abolishing most of these rules. Over time and with a different set of incentives, the states might decide to restore certain prerogatives to party leaders. This restoration would take the form of a process that would emerge from the bottom. However, given the fact that nationalization of party rules has already done so much to erode the power of parties, I believe in this case that certain positive actions may be required of the national political parties, some of which are included in the Miller Center's report on the presidential nominating process. But the general principal to which we should try to adhere is a simple one. To the extent possible, the means should be consistent with the ends. And if the end is a system of relatively strong parties that grow up from the local level, we should look for a process of change in which the states and state parties play a key role. It would be most unwise to rely upon the federal government to do the job of restoring the power of political parties.

Second, we should begin to think about *attacking the system of primary elections,* not only at the level of national politics, that is in presidential primaries, but at the state and local levels. In the state of Virginia today, many of our officials are nominated without primary elections, and the system seems to be working quite well. Democracy has not been threatened, and the parties have been able to exercise significant power. So why not the slogan, "As Virginia Goes, So Goes The Nation"? It is my view that we can never hope to restore the vitality of our parties until we restore to them the crucial function of nominating.

Third, I would *alter the campaign finance legislation.* We must look for changes that remove the perverse incentives for money to flow into political action committees rather than into the hands of political parties or candidates. It is on this point, in fact, that we find one of the great ironies of reform. Under the impact of campaign finance laws, which were designed to limit the influence of interest groups, we have in fact seen that the influence of interest groups has become all the greater. What is to be done? Some reformers want us to look for ways to get around the Constitution by creating yet new forms of legislation to restrict the contributions of political action committees. I would prefer, however, that we attempt to resolve the problem by fewer, rather than more, regulations. I would prefer to place the limit on campaign contributions by individuals at a much higher level than presently exists, as a way of depreciating the relative importance of contributions from political action committees. I would prefer to remove all spending limitations in presidential primaries and presidential election campaigns, thereby allowing candidates to raise money above that provided by public financing. This step again would devalue the activity of political action committees. Finally, I would allow political parties to contribute to their candidates, national and local, to a much higher level than is presently allowed.

Fourth, it is probably time to *challenge some Supreme Court decisions* which have made it virtually illegal for states and localities to include elements of patronage in local politics. In a most amazing decision of the Supreme Court, *Elrod v. Burns,* First Amendment rights were interpreted in such a way as to give government officials a certain property in office so that

17

they could not be fired by an incoming political party. I call this amazing because from the time of Andrew Jackson through William Jennings Bryant, one of the most important questions in American politics was whether there should be property in office, and the Democratic party had always held that there should not be. Now, however, the Court comes along, and, in line with the tradition of reform, quickly disposes of this issue in terms of a First Amendment right. What is all the more amazing is the contradictory view of the reformers on constitutional interpretation. They possess the orthodoxy of Jerry Falwell when it comes to looking for ways to avoid the constitutional limitations on campaign finance legislation. But they have the promiscuity of a Hugh Hefner when it comes to interpreting First Amendment rights with respect to party patronage.

Finally, I would suggest that we begin to think again about *methods of changing our ballot and ballot laws.* In the nineteenth century, the states did not print the ballots. The ballots were ordinarily printed by the political parties, and citizens would take their ballots with them into the ballot booth and hand them over to the officials. Of course, in this age we cannot go back exactly to that kind of system. But I certainly would not be adverse to a system of standardized tickets, which political parties could print and which individuals could bring into the ballot box. What I have in mind is a pre-punched computer card that could be fed into a voting machine. The citizen would have the option, if he or she preferred, to bring a ballot printed by the political party, as distinct from using the state's ballot. This would avoid a great many ballot access problems that faced a candidate like John Anderson and that have plagued electoral politics at the state and local level for so long. It would allow for fusion tickets at the state and local levels—that is, third or splinter parties nominating certain candidates of the other parties for offices—and it therefore might stimulate more political participation. I do not in principle favor steps that encourage splinter parties, but I think it is unwise for states to erect artificial barriers to close them out. The legitimacy of the major parties in running their own affairs can only be defended if the electoral system as a whole is open to new parties. I would much prefer to see closed parties and an open electoral system than open parties and a closed electoral system.

These, I admit, are modest reforms. But I began with the question of how we achieve political salvation. For some time now everyone has thought it was by a direct path through reform to heaven. But politics, alas, is not religion, and the way to salvation in politics may not be through Saint Peter's gate. Thank you.

THE HISTORY of the PRESIDENTIAL NOMINATING PROCESS

Douglass Cater

MR. THOMPSON: We are pleased to welcome you to the second George Gund lecture on the presidential nominating process. The George Gund Foundation is a Cleveland foundation which has made possible, not only this lecture series, but also the work of the Miller Center Commission on the Presidential Nominating Process.

It is a rare personal as well as professional privilege to welcome Douglass Cater as our second Gund lecturer. Doug Cater was special assistant to President Lyndon B. Johnson and Secretary of the Cabinet in the Johnson administration. He is the founder of the Aspen Institute program on communication in society. He is the author of numerous books, including *The Fourth Branch of Government* and *The Powers of Government.* He was an editor of *The Reporter* magazine. He has served on numerous commissions, including the first commission of the Miller Center concerned with the presidential press conference. Those of us who have known Douglass Cater over the years were not surprised about a year ago when he initiated an Aspen Institute inquiry into the presidential nominating process. He proceeded, as he has throughout much of his career, to seek to tap the best knowledge and insights to be found on the subject. He established a round robin—not a letter writing effort, but an effort to share longer papers by people who had a keen interest in this subject. One of the seeds fell on fertile soil and in part the initiative of the Miller Center was inspired by some of the early papers which Doug Cater and the Aspen Institute distributed in their project on the nominating process.

Mr. Cater is now President Cater, president of Washington College in Chestertown, Maryland. He without any doubt will continue commenting, writing, and thinking about public affairs as he has throughout his career. And we feel particularly fortunate that he should be with us today to give the second Gund lecture. It is an honor and privilege to introduce Douglass Cater.

MR. CATER: It is a privilege to be in this majestic room on this marvelous campus designed by one of our founding fathers to speak on a topic, the choosing of our President, which I believe is both timely and holds historical relevance. I was delighted this past week that Art Buchwald was recognized as not just a humorous commentator but as a man of political insight. Some years ago he wrote the very trenchant observation that, unless Americans convene every four years to choose a leader, the country will revert to the Indians. He was trying to point out that in the choosing of our President we are not only electing a man—or perhaps someday a woman—but are reaffirming our nationhood. The process itself is important to the kind of government and, indeed, the kind of nation we are.

We are in a serious predicament. The drive for a more perfect democracy in America has led to excesses of the electoral process that could bring a crisis of governance—a crisis in which the leader chosen by the process may not have the credibility which the process is meant to ensure. Henry Kissinger remarked at one public gathering that the job of President today can only be considered by unemployed egomaniacs. (Of course, the Constitution stipulates that they have to be born in this country.) The last two contests have given indication that we are approaching the condition of the "perpetual campaign" engaged in by professional candidates. The choosing of the President has come a long way from the intent of our founding fathers.

In tracing the debate at the Constitutional Convention over choosing the leader, one finds that it was characterized by irresolution. The founding fathers had no agreement in the beginning or even well into their deliberations whether they wished a unitary head of government or leadership by council, or what would be the length of term. Should such a leader or leaders be available for reelection? And, most important of all, what would be the method by which this leader or leaders would be chosen?

The confusion is reflected in the notes on the convention. From May to September the debate went back and forth with a great deal of passing of resolutions and subsequent revoking of the resolutions. At least three times the convention voted that

22

the selection should be made by Congress, and three times this was subsequently rejected. Governor Morris, of New Jersey, comparing election by Congress to the election of the Pope, said that it would be a work of intrigue, of cabal, and of faction. Edmund Randolph of Virginia, quite early in the debate, said that he favored election by the people, "at least in theory." George Mason, of Virginia, responded resoundingly with the warning which still rings in our ears,

> It would be as unnatural to refer the choice of a proper character for chief magistrate to the people as it would to refer a trial of colours to a blind man. The extent of the country renders it impossible that the people can have the requisite capacity to judge the respective pretentions of the candidates.

Three times the convention chose the method of election by Congress and three times they rejected it. As for length of office, the delegates voted at least once for a six year term, taking heed of Roger Ellsworth's admonition that "there must be duties of the President which will make him unpopular." Rufus King took this argument to the limit by proposing that the President should occupy office for the median life of princes, which he reckoned to be twenty years. Mr. Wilson solemnly responded that "we would be rejecting the man in the prime of his life, cast aside like a useless hulk." Elbridge Gerry, of Massachusetts, remarked sadly, "We seem to be entirely at a loss on this matter."

Ben Franklin, the patriarch of the convention, came forth with an interesting proposal, arguing at length that the chief executive should receive no salary but should be reimbursed for necessary expenses in the manner that George Washington had been compensated during his eight years as commander in chief of the continental armies. Otherwise, Franklin warned, ". . . the combining of ambition and avarice would attract men of strong passions and indefatigable activity in their own selfish pursuit." George Washington, who was presiding officer at the convention, failing to connect on Franklin's proposal which, Madison records in his journal, was "treated with great respect but rather for the author of it than from any apparent conviction of its expediency or its practicality."

And so the Constitutional Convention floundered until September when the Committee of Eleven, consisting of a member from each state, reported out a plan that bore remarkable resemblance to the final document: First, each state would

23

have the privilege of deciding by what method it would choose electors. (It was the first time the elector was seriously considered.) Second, the electors would not meet in a common place but would convene in the separate states. (Madison felt that this separation of the electors would help prevent the opportunity for cabal or corruption.) Each elector would cast two ballots. (Since it was not specified which ballot was for which office, this led to the 1800 electoral crisis when Thomas Jefferson and Aaron Burr held a tie vote and the contest had to be taken to the House of Representatives.) No member of Congress or federal office holder could serve as an elector (thus rejecting any notion of a quasi-parliamentary approach). When there was no clear majority of electoral votes, the Committee of Eleven proposed that the Senate would make the choice. (Since it was feared that the Senate would be "too aristocratic," the delegates turned over the choice to the House of Representatives.) The President would hold a four year term but would have no written bar to multiple reelections. The notion of an advisory council repeatedly raised by Madison was rejected, prompting George Mason to conclude sadly, "The President will be unsupported by proper information and advice, and will generally be directed by minions and favorites."

Clearly, the founding fathers intended a quasi-deliberative process for choosing the President. They intended that the elector be a thinking person. Yet they also stipulated that electors would not convene in one place and made no provision for a second electoral tally in the event of failure to achieve a majority in the first. In turning the decision over to the House of Representatives, each state would vote as a single unit no matter how divided its congressmen happened to be. No electoral role was specified for ordinary citizens unless the state legislature decided to define one.

Alexander Hamilton was able to write in Federalist Paper No. 68, "The mode of the appointment of the chief magistrate of the United States is almost the only part of the constitutional system which has escaped without severe censure or which has received the slightest mark of approbation from its opponents." Hamilton claimed four major benefits for the electoral college system. It would permit the choice of a President to be "made by persons who are most capable of analyzing the qualities adapted to the station of the presidency and most likely to possess the information and discernment requisite to such complicated investigations." Second, it promised to make the executive independent for his continuance in office of all but the people themselves. He would not be answerable either to the Congress or to the state governments. Third, it would reduce the opportunity for "tumult and disorder." Members of the electoral college convening in their separate states would have a hard time reflecting the "heats and ferments" of the people. This detached and divided situation, in Hamilton's words, ". . . would raise an obstacle to cabal, intrigue and corruption since the college would come into being for the sole purpose of choosing a president and vice president and would then promptly dissolve." Hamilton concluded,

> The process of election affords a moral certainty that the Office of President will seldom fall to the lot of any man who is not in eminent degree endowed with the requisite qualifications. Talents for low intrigue and the little arts of popularity may alone suffice to elevate a man to the first honors in a single state but it will require other talents and a different kind of merit to establish him in the esteem and confidence of the whole union.

This system as devised by the founding fathers has worked only three times in our history. During the first two elections there was an uncontested father of our country in the person of George Washington. By 1796, faction has begun to rear its head when the incipient Democratic Republican party began to assert itself against the dominant Federalist party. Thomas Jefferson came within three votes of defeating John Adams in the electoral college. By 1800, as mentioned earlier, Jefferson and Burr, both in the same party, received identical votes. It required thirty six ballots in the House of Representatives to reach a decision. According to both Jefferson and friends of Burr, there were great temptations to corruption in this extended contest.

In 1824, an event occurred that had not been foreseen: Andrew Jackson, though receiving more electoral votes, lost to John Quincy Adams. The suspicions of corruption when Adams subsequently appointed Henry Clay as his minister of state did lasting damage to Adams' period as President.

By 1836, only South Carolina had not extended the choice of the electors to the popular vote. Most states adopted the winner-take-all method of choice which meant that the elector was not chosen for his individual qualities but only to cast a rubber stamp vote for the popular choice of President. This has never been clearly specified, resulting very rarely in the phenomenon of the runaway elector. Twice since then there has been a difference between the popular and the electoral college vote. Typically, the electoral vote reinforces and often exaggerates the size of victory represented in the popular vote. There have been a number of times when a President has been elected with less than a majority of the popular vote.

In 1876, a crisis resulted when the votes of three southern states were challenged. Congress provided for the establishment of an election commission, an action, by the way, nowhere specified in the Constitution. The commission split strictly according to the partisan division of its members. Finally, Hays prevailed over Tilden in the House of Representatives after a compromise was reached ending the era of reconstruction in the south.

During the 20th century, there have been three narrow escapes from throwing the election into the House of Representatives. In 1912, Roosevelt received enough votes to defeat Taft and elect Woodrow Wilson. In 1948, Henry Wallace challenged Harry Truman but failed to get enough votes to cause an electoral college impasse. Then, in 1968, George Wallace required affidavits from electors pledged to him that they would vote as he directed after the election. He could have bargained with the two front runners but he failed to achieve enough electoral votes. (A switch of a few thousand votes in a few southern or border states could have made this strategy successful.) The risk of going into the House of Representatives continued in our latest election when John Anderson, as a "third force" candidate, might have received enough electoral votes to prevent either of the major nominees from receiving a clear electoral majority.

To examine the struggle for the choice of leader one must go beyond the electoral college. In 1831, de Tocqueville made his celebrated tour of this country and wrote afterward,

> For a long time before the appointed time has come the election becomes the important and, so to speak, the all engrossing topic of discussion. Factional order is redoubled and all the artificial passions which the imagination can create in a happy and peaceful land are agitated and brought to light. It is true that as soon as the choice is determined this order is dispelled. Calm returns and the river which had nearly broken its bank sinks to its usual level. But who can refrain from astonishment that such a storm should have arisen in the first place?

26

The struggle, as I indicated, could not be confined to the formal electoral system. By 1800 we find the beginnings of King Caucus in which partisans in Congress came together in order to put up their favorite for the office and determine who would be the competitors in the subsequent electoral process. By 1831, the first national party convention took place when the Republicans gathered together to nominate Henry Clay. A year later, the first Democratic Convention, which had no problem of selecting a nominee for President since they were supporting incumbent Andrew Jackson, worked their will to discard Jackson's vice president, John C. Calhoun, and to replace him with Martin Van Buren.

For the rest of the 19th century the nominating process was dominated by national party conventions within a predominantly two party system. Advocates argued that the national party convention, despite its appearance of disarray, was indeed a very good intermediating institution for reaching consensus and choosing the person best able to lead the party and prospectively, the nation. Detractors pointed to the abundant evidence that boss rule, conducted in smoke-filled rooms, often dominated the convention.

By 1901, discontent with the national party convention led to the first presidential primary which took place in Florida. By 1912, fifteen states had provisions for presidential primaries. Then the primary system went into a period of decline. As late as 1960, there were only three significant state primaries, leading to the choice of John F. Kennedy over Hubert H. Humphrey. The tide toward primaries turned full strength. By 1980, we had 36 primaries in this country which successfully locked up the nominations of both major party contenders well before the conventions had opened. Yet, despite their decline in role, national party conventions had almost doubled in size over the last two decades. There had been a noticeable decline in role and indeed, even in presence of traditional party leaders and professionals from the various states: the governors, senators, congressmen, and mayors who had in the past played center stage in the national conventions. We had, by 1980, approached a condition of "King Primary" rather than "King Convention" or "King Caucus." In 1968, forty percent of the delegates at the convention were chosen in primaries. In 1980, nearly three quarters of the delegates were selected in the primaries and represented slates of "instructed messengers" who without room for maneuver, locked up the nominations before the convention even opened.

Let us examine a best case-worst case comparison of the presidential selection process as it exists today. From the best case perspective, we continue every four years to hold presidential elections in confident expectation that we will emerge with a leader and that the nation, as Tocqueville mentioned so many years ago, will calm down once again. No other society in the world can make that boast over so long a period. The system has had to adapt to a changing environment. With railroads, with highways, with airplanes, and, most recently, with the electronic communications system, one would be foolish to cry over the fact that the modern day election is not like it was in the 19th century. Today, television brings the contest into every household and there is a greater opportunity for many more millions to observe, to judge, and to participate in the electoral process. Of course, the best case advocate would admit, this is not a tidy contest. But it does require skilled leadership to organize the necessary forces to win such a contest. It permits the unknown or the lesser known candidate to get into the process early enough that he can acquire name recognition and the possibility of winning the nomination, as Jimmy Carter did in 1976. It shakes up the stratification of the bureaucracy of politics. The extended campaign tests the stamina of the candidates and fulfills Woodrow Wilson's stipulation that a President has to be an athlete if he is to survive the office. Some advocates would argue that our electoral system, with all its excuses, represents a mysterious communion between the candidates and the people.

Let us turn to the "worst case" arguments. The first would be that the election no longer serves its intended purposes. It discourages the experienced leaders from getting into the contest and it attracts raw beginners. It substitutes form for substance. The hasty handshake and the even hastier argument replaces the serious dialogue. Our campaigning has become a marathon; it distracts too much attention from the serious business of governing. The President finds himself, before he is well into his first term in office, having to turn his attention to the problems of reelection. It is producing "professional candidates," meaning that the candidate is more to be noted for his attention to the business of campaigning than to the business of leadership. And it closes off others prematurely, so that quite often the exaggerated publicity that goes with the primary contest makes it impossible for able senators or governors busy with affairs of office to get into the contest at a later stage. We all become preoccupied with the techniques and the tactics rather than the broad strategy of the leader.

The argument is also made that it corrupts the candidates. They do not wait for the courtship of their peers, but arrogantly make the decision to go for the presidency with very little evidence of a gestation process. The life of a candidate is no longer one that cultivates the qualities of leadership. He is a new type and is surrounded by new types of camp followers: the media advisors, the public opinion experts—these have replaced the traditional advisory stable. He becomes adept at posturing for the media. Even when he goes to the grass roots in New Hampshire or elsewhere, the emphasis is not on the direct contact with the voter but how it is going to play on the evening television news. It turns the candidate into a loner in party politics. He no longer relies or is relied upon by the national or state parties. He is cut off from serious and sustained party support once he needs it in office.

The primary does not represent the true voice of the people. The people are being asked to give their support to a particular individual well before they have had the opportunity to make up their minds. Persistent, organized minorities play an excessive role in the primary process. Our nation's politics, even in the area of foreign affairs, becomes hostage to partisan maneuvering. The most outrageous claims and counter claims are made particularly when one of the candidates is an incumbent in the White House. For a sustained period of time, every four years, the nation is exposed and vulnerable while it goes through this contest for the choosing of the President.

A good many people have begun to take note and to be concerned about the problem. Important studies have been made and commissions have evaluated the process. There is a remarkable consensus, resulting from these various deliberative groups. No one believes that a single reform can miraculously restore order to the electoral process. It did not reach the present chaos by deliberate design. Recent reforms, with the best of intentions, have unwittingly contributed to the present predicament. Campaign financing controls enacted into law and interpreted by the Supreme Court have led to an outrageous condition in which candidates and their committees and the party committees are limited quite stringently in support funds while independent political action committees, claiming no relationship to particular candidates, can raise and spend unlimited amounts. Shrewd manipulators of politics have seen this glaring gap in our governance. Over the last four years there has been an amazing increase in the number of independent political action committees and the sums contributed to them. It permits a committee to support a candidate on grounds that the candidate himself has not professed. It reduces even further the role that national political parties can play in the funding of politics.

Those who have looked at our present predicament have pointed to the dangers of extremist approaches. There is no possibility to return to the pure electoral college model established by the founding fathers. Nor would it be wise to move toward a plebiscitary democracy. Let us take the farthest step by holding national primaries every four years. There is a need to strike a balance. We should not attempt to eliminate the primaries, but they should, by party rule and if necessary by act of Congress, be curtailed in their duration to no more than a three month period during the time prior to the conventions. The intent would be to cluster state primaries so that a number would fall on the same day and thereby reduce the publicity focused on a single primary.

Balance would come by reducing the power of the slates of instructed delegates and by restoring a role for the "thinking delegate"—one still free when he gets to the national convention to consider how he will cast his vote. A role would also be restored for elected and party leaders in the delegations at the national conventions.

There are other concerns that need to be addressed as we conduct this bicentennial review of how we choose our President. I am concerned about the increase in size of the national conventions. Once they get beyond a certain size they are bound to become circuses and television coverage further emphasizes the circus-like quality. It would not reduce the representative nature of the conventions if they were shrunk to half their present size. The conventions can be better restricted to serious business rather than clowning and grandstanding. At the British conventions, party leaders and candidates sit on the dais throughout the major debates and participate freely. We need to find ways to develop greater informality of debates rather than to suffer the Valhalla syndrome of the convention today with the speaker so raised above the throng below that no one below hears or cares what he has to say. We need to consider better techniques of registering voting or public sentiment during the preconvention contest. One proposal for what is called "approval voting" during the primaries would permit citizens to vote for two or more candidates. In this way the voter would be avoiding prematurely declaring for a single individual. The proposal deserves serious consideration and possibly testing in the next primaries.

We need to look once more at whether we think the electoral college system any longer has meaning. There have been proposals to reform the electoral college by dividing up a state's votes rather than winner-take-all within each state. Some have proposed (and both Nixon and Carter have supported these proposals) to abolish the electoral college and allow the outcome of the popular election to be decisive. Abolition would require a constitutional amendment and we are far away from any great popular impulse to rewrite that provision of the Constitution.

In Tibet when the Dalai Lama dies the priests begin a search for the infant into whom the soul of the deceased leader has migrated. Americans would argue that this is a very mystical way to find a successor to take over leadership. Yet if the Tibetans were to examine how we go about choosing a leader they might claim that ours is an even more mystical process. One of the more thoughtful analysts of the American presidency, Professor Richard Neustadt of Harvard, wrote to me before the outcome of the 1980 election:

> I agree with your worst case analysis. Indeed, I take the worst case in this instance to be the reasonably likely one. Professional candidates campaign almost permanently in a mode quite unlike governing, and it spells cumulative trouble for a political system always prone to civil war and now under the constant if repressed threat of a nuclear war by mutual miscalculation.
> Ours is a constitutional monarchy, a real one not a mere symbol. And it is as though hereditary chemistry condemned us to a series of defective kings. This is precisely what the republican institutions ought to spare us. It should not be beyond the wit of man to make them serve.

We are at a stage in our history when we must decide whether we move even further toward direct democracy or we return toward what was intended by the founding fathers—representative democracy. Television tempts us to go the whole way with direct democracy. We can create a Greek marketplace with television allowing the citizen to sit in his living room, observe his leaders, and register his verdict. Interactive television could make possible an instant plebiscite on the particular issue of the day. Indeed, one might not even need a President. Simply a tabulator of the plebiscites. We see that in the present evolution of the electoral process there are abundant signs of citizen disaffection. More than three decades into the television era, it is surprising that we experience continuing decline in the percentage of voters who turn out for presidential elections. The decline is even more marked among those who turn out for other elections. The way we select our Presidents not only determines which individual will lead but also the talents and the temperament of leadership. Pursuing the present course we frustrate the business of governing even as we try to select a governor.

PART TWO

THE POLITICAL PROCESS, POLITICAL PARTIES and the NOMINATING PROCESS

THE PRESIDENT, THE PUBLIC and the NOMINATING PROCESS
Senator Eugene McCarthy

MR. THOMPSON: We are pleased to welcome you to a Miller Center Forum with Senator Eugene McCarthy. Adlai Stevenson used to say that if the voters of the world had participated in the presidential election, he would have won by a landslide. If the voters of Minnesota for the Senate are as responsive as some of you who have assembled here from the state of Virginia, Senator McCarthy ought to be optimistic.

We are pleased that Senator McCarthy could join us today for a discussion of the presidency and the nominating process. He was a member of the Miller Center Commission that examined this question. It will surprise none of you who have known Senator McCarthy over the years that he has his own independent judgement on some of the points that were discussed by the Commission. I think we are fortunate that he will talk with us today about the subject.

Some of you already know that Senator McCarthy is a graduate of St. John's College; that he worked in the War Department and at one stage in Military Intelligence; that he served in the House and in the Senate; that he held important committee posts; that he ran for the presidency of the United States; and that he remains a poet and writer. But his first love has been from earliest days, both as a scholar and practitioner, the study and practice of politics.

Therefore, we feel fortunate Senator McCarthy has been able to take a little time from a busy schedule during a visit to the University of Virginia, and will talk with us about the nominating process, about the presidency and personality cults, and about any other subject that he may see fit to introduce in his prepared statement.

SENATOR MCCARTHY: Well, I am prepared to make seven or eight rash judgments in the course of this talk. I have explained why I really ran for the presidency in 1968. I got tired of the liberal commentators explaining it in terms of some kind of psychological disorder. They don't like to make moral judgments because that's their way of being kind; they just say you're neurotic or paranoid. And the conservatives—I was rather attracted to them because they attributed rather traditional vices to me—like hatred and envy. And one of them said it was enmity. I had sort of forgotten about enmity. It's a good biblical word. It's sort of between vice and virtue and I've been practicing that ever since. I have more enmity than anybody, but I say I really did it to get my poetry published. Poets will do anything to get published. I tell young people who ask, "Say, how do we get published?" I say, "Well, you can run for the presidency." It's a hard way to go and you may be subjected to political criticism in your poetry that you would not otherwise be subjected to.

The whole question of how we pick presidential candidates and pick presidents, I think, is a most serious one, and I have four or five ideas about it. Having once been rejected by the Democratic party for another candidate favoring the continuation of the Vietnam War, you have to believe there is something wrong with the system. And then having run against Jimmy Carter and Gerald Ford and lost again, you are even more convinced there is something wrong with the system. There is no other way to explain how that could have happened to you, if you want to come out of the cave again.

But beyond that there are three or four things that bear upon it and I am serious about all of these. I'll mention three that are somewhat negative. I think they're important but I don't know what you would do about them. One, I think the process would be helped if we eliminated the vice presidential office so you would not have the nominating process cluttered up with vice presidential candidates. It has two bad effects: One, if you pick a person who really is qualified to be President, it's a shame to waste him for four years or eight years; you can actually destroy him in the office. And if the person isn't qualified he ought not to be put in a position where he would succeed to it. I would much rather have us follow something like the provisions of the Twenty-Sixth Amendment, if we did it, of Congress picking for us. It's not difficult if the President dies or is disabled to set up an easy procedure whereby the Congress could pick a successor, instead of setting up this office which, as I say, has one danger in it: you waste good people. We would have been better off if Lyndon Johnson had been majority leader during the Kennedy administration than vice president. I think we would have been better off if Humphrey had been in the Senate instead of vice president. I don't know about some of the later ones. Walter Mondale is a little unhappy with me because I said he had the soul of a vice president. I thought it was high praise. What do you want him to have? I mean, to want him to have more or less would be wrong; it would seem to me just right. But it does confuse the campaign and also it complicates an administration. I see Griffin Bell has just said having Mondale there complicated his administration of the Justice Department. If he hadn't been there it wouldn't have happened. Whether Bell's judgment is right or not, I don't know. It really wasn't so bad until they'd (Mondale and his staff) cluttered up the campaign, but after that it was sort of accepted that they would be quiet.

Beginning with Eisenhower and Nixon, they got into this thing of giving new meaning to the office. No one ever said that before. You didn't try; you'd just stay there and wait. But Nixon was going to be given new functions, and you may remember when Eisenhower was asked when Nixon was running, what Nixon had done, he said, "Give me a couple of weeks." Kennedy supposedly said that Lyndon was consulted on everything that worked out well, and things that didn't work out he either hadn't consulted him or hadn't taken his advice. Humphrey said he was very happy, but in his memoirs he said it was really a bad relationship with Johnson. So it has sort of run on down.

I was considered for a while for the vice president by Johnson in 1964, and I took myself out at a certain point when Johnson said he was going to give new meaning to the office. I said I was willing to take it pretty much on the Jeffersonian basis. Jefferson said it was a good office. He said it gave him time in the winter for philosophical reflections, and in the summer to contemplate nature. Actually, while he was vice president Jefferson invented a leather buggy top. He got a prize for designing a new clock and he invented a hemp beater, and supposedly conceived the dollar, the dime, and the penny. That's a pretty constructive vice presidency. That was sort of what I had in mind. The office clutters it up.

The second negative is we ought to abolish the federal election law, that procedure. It was a violent intrusion of the political process in this country and pretty well done in the name of reform. As a result of it there are three bad things that have come of it with the court interpretation: One, it gives a tremen-

37

dous advantage to a person who has personal wealth. The court has said an individual or his family can spend as much of their own money as they want—ten, twenty, thirty million dollars. But if you have someone who does not have money he cannot accept a personal contribution of more than a thousand dollars, which is a very strange interpretation of freedom of speech —to say that the candidate who has money can spend as much as he wants but someone else, who might want to spend money to exercise his freedom of speech in a community action, cannot do it. So there is that first point.

We haven't seen it quite at the presidential level yet, but certainly in congressional elections in two ways: the limitations on contributions and then the limitations on outside income once you're in office. It means that progressively, the Congress and the Senate are filling up with foundations, brand names— Heinz fifty-seven varieties. They are people whose grand-parents wouldn't trust them with their money, and even under the fourth generation sew this guy up in a trust. So now we put him in the Senate, and he's got our money. We should say, "God, if your grandfather wouldn't trust you, why should we?" But it's a special advantage and part of it comes out of the federal election system. Congress had a big debate last week, two days, on this whole question of congressional salaries, how much outside income could you have and could you deduct $75 a day. I thought someone should have proposed that any-one who comes into the Senate should be required to contri-bute his whole foundation—just sell what you have and give to the poor; come follow me. You'd be surprised at how many would have left the room at that point.

The second is the development of the power of corporate political action committees, which the Federal Election Law provided for. In 1980, $130 million was contributed by politi-cal action committees. What is wrong with that? There are two things wrong with it: one, I think they are impersonal; and the second is that progressively the whole of politics, both Demo-crats and Republicans, those in office begin to be informed by whatever the corporate soul is, which has limited economic liability but also limited social, moral, and political liability. You can have a whole political structure which is inspired so far as it is only by the limitation of a corporate soul. I would rather be in a political situation, such as in one of the examples that was used in support of reform which was the Nixon cam-paign of 1972, in which they said, "Look at Nixon, he got two and a half million dollars from Clement Stone. Think of that, isn't that terrible?" First of all, I would rather have a candidate who got $2.5 million from someone identified as Clement Stone than $2.5 million from some vague corporate PAC; you don't know what the PAC is, who it is, what it represents. It's something less than a full person. And you knew what Clement Stone was. Think of the outside influence on Nixon, you say; well, think of it. What's so bad about that? Any outside influence on Nixon would probably be great. You get these silly arguments; they don't follow through. They think of the outside influence on Richard Nixon; you know it's a terrible prospect. It was a carrying argument, but as I say, the Clement Stone thing was real and you could identify it, but progressively the PAC thing becomes anonymous and impersonal and it operates from a moral, intellectual and social base which is less than that which you might get from a person who made it.

The third—and it's involved in this—is federal financing which is inherently so dangerous. The idea that you could have a political process which is controlled and financed by the government itself, the government which it is intended to establish, is a closed circuit. The government controls the process by which the government is to be chosen which was essentially the procedure in Germany, and still is I guess, when Hitler was elected. Goebbels was supposed to have said, "Now we've got it, because we can control the political process." So they had broken into this closed circuit and could control it. You say, well, not all people will do it, but some people will. To accept government financing is absurd. If this proposition had been brought into the constitutional convention they would have run them out. They'd say, "What are you talking about, having the government control and finance the process by which the government itself is to be chosen?" It would have been so contrary to the whole conception of open politics through which politics was to be conducted and government established, it would not have been allowed, it seems to me, in Constitution Hall or Independence Hall. That's sort of the negative.

On the positive side there are the things you've addressed yourselves to here. What are party rules? If we have an open system in which we could have five or six parties and more than that, which the Constitution anticipated meant really no parties, which means an unlimited number of parties, this would not be so important. But once you have legalized two political parties, which is what we really have done in the Federal Election Law and in the laws of most states, politics is channeled into two parties. It doesn't necessarily have to be Republican and Democratic, but formally in fact it is. I think if that continues you'd then have to have some national rules for party procedures reflecting maybe the principle of one man, one vote or full participation—something other than the quota system which was the Democratic proposal of 1972. If you're going to use quotas you might just keep running the computers until only one name comes out; that would be the ultimate distribution of selection. You were supposed to get the most average person for President which might be better than what we are doing with the rational process that we're following now. Theoretically that would be the projection of it.

As an example, the rules of the Democratic party in the last four conventions determined who was nominated. Had the 1972 rules applied in 1968 the convention would have turned out differently. The 1968 rules were supposedly the old rules of accommodation in which there was no accommodation in 1968. They changed the rules in 1972 with McGovern as chairman of the commission, and the 1972 rules were just right for McGovern. He could not have been nominated with the 1968 rules or the 1976 rules, in which they had two things: one, that they abolished the unit rule in non-primary states but kept the winner-take-all primary. So he got his share in the nonprimary states but he got everything in the winner-take-all primaries: a clear contradiction in principle. Humphrey didn't have much of a case because when we argued the same way in 1968, he said he didn't want to do a democratic thing by undemocratic ways, which holds up a lot of possibilities. We said, "Would you like to do a democratic thing by democratic ways or would you like to do an undemocratic thing by democratic ways?" You'd force him to give you the final answer. But by 1972 Humphrey was willing to do the democratic thing by undemocratic ways, which was to say you should not have a winner-take-all primary, which is absolutely right.

Then they changed the rules again because of inequity, and Jimmy Carter was on the commission. And Carter could not have been nominated with the '72 rules because Carter had his share of all the primaries and he didn't need the unit rule because he had the solid South anyway plus the Baptists and a few others. So he didn't have to worry about the unit rule in non-primary states because he had them all anyway. But he got his share in the primary states. Well, he didn't think he could win in '80 with that rule so they changed the rules in '78, in anticipation of the convention of 1980, and that was when they introduced the threshold concept. The liberals thought it was wonderful. Jimmy asked for twenty-five percent threshold first and they compromised at fifteen percent which was all he needed—just like Brer Rabbit, you know. He'd get twenty-five percent. They say to be a successful peanut processor you have to think small. The liberals were having grand views of it whereas he was counting it. The principle was, if you got less than twenty-five percent in a caucus state or primary state you didn't get anything. They then backed it down to fifteen percent. For example, Governor Brown got fourteen percent, I think, in Maine. If he had gotten one percent more he would have had three or four delegates, but he didn't get any. Then the delegates you didn't get were thrown into a pool which were then reassigned to people who got over fifteen percent. Well, you could figure that an incumbent president was likely to get over fifteen percent every place and maybe over thirty percent, and he's going to win some. So when you got through with it, with the threshold and the reallocation, why he was almost certain to have at least fifty-one percent, which he did have. I think you have to give him credit. It was not accidental; he figured it out.

So now they changed the rules again for 1984. I don't know quite what they put into them but this will mean in one, two, three, four, five successive times—there was no way of anticipating what would happen in terms of what the rules were at the previous convention. And I say, if politics is open so you could organize your own party, go ahead. You'd say, "Well, why worry about the process if you have your own party?" But when it is limited to two parties and the rules of the parties, Republicans and Democrats, determine in effect the process through the rules, who is going to be nominated, who we are going to have a chance to vote for? One of two. Then I think you have to look to those procedures, as a basis for trying to clear up the process. And that's really what you have been talking about.

There are four or five ways to proceed: one is to go back to the old caucus system, which is better than what we have now. We had a primary in Minnesota, I think it was adopted in 1940, maybe it was 1944, about that time. It was set as the earliest major primary in the hope that Harold Stassen could win one primary. Finally, in 1952 it was tested, and Eisenhower beat him in the Minnesota primary, and then in 1956 Estes Kefauver beat Stevenson in the Minnesota primary, and we were all supporting Stevenson, the party was. So the Republicans and Democrats both decided in 1958 that the primary was a bad idea and we abolished it and went back to the old caucus system. I say I think the caucuses would probably be better than what we have.

Of the various other proposals, the worst thing would be a national primary. I tell you what we do in this country—if something doesn't work well on a limited scale we say "let's nationalize." It's like you educators—there was a controversy, was it last year?—about the so-called standardized testing. What they said was, well the tests are not reliable, the Stanford tests aren't, the Harcourt Brace tests aren't, and the Princeton tests aren't, so someone said, "Why don't we have a national test?" So instead of having three or four testing procedures, each of which was reasonably unreliable, we would have a national one which was certainly unreliable. That's about the same principle involved in proposing a national primary. People say: well, we have too many primaries, the primaries don't work, they give the media too much power. So you say, why don't we nationalize it? And you say, well, it's rather obvious as to why we shouldn't do it for various reasons—things we have observed with the proliferation of primaries and with the growing power of national media.

I am a little sensitive to that. When I was running as an Independent in 1976 we brought an action against the networks on the grounds that the fairness and equal time doctrine had been violated. CBS testified that I had been given twenty-two minutes in four months, which they thought was —most of it was morning and noon—as much as I deserved. I had been mentioned twice on Cronkite in four months. Both of those had been negative. But in any case, we pointed out that in the same four months Cronkite had two stories about an ape boy. Walter had come on one night and said, "We've just found a boy raised by the apes" and he was very excited. And he said "That's the way it is." And six weeks later Cronkite came on and said, "We've discovered that the boy we said was raised by the apes was not raised by the apes," and he was just as excited. Another damn discovery. And he said, "That's the way it is." And we argued that we thought we deserved as much attention because Walter was calling me a spoiler, you know. And if you're a spoiler why people ought to know why you're doing it or how you're spoiling it. We actually did say in the testimony that we suspected that CBS hadn't told the whole truth in the retraction which was the fact that the kid had liberal parents and they had made him watch Walter Cronkite every night since he was four years old and that in effect was indistinguishable from what Walter thought he had discovered the first time he came on.

I would actually think we'd be better off if we could ban television political ads altogether and then enforce the equal time and fairness doctrine. And if it drove them to not covering political news I think the country would be better off. There'd be no real loss. We don't allow them to advertise cigarettes and alcohol, so maybe we ought to ban political ads and go to the other end of the spectrum. I'd like to see religious ads banned and also political ads. I really think the evangelists should not be allowed to appeal for funds on television. You can come on and preach if you want to but no appeals for funds, no selling of the Bible, and I think politics is the same way. We'd really be better off if we forced people to make political judgments either on what they read or on what they hear instead of what you get now. On the news you get a hype on everything that's presented and then if you allow political ads with props and sound effects, with charts and flashing lights, people can't possibly make a rational decision. And, if you can't handle the media, the thing to do is to stop using it. Let's make political decisions under different circumstances and with different considerations. It really is pretty bad.

Actually, I did make a scientific study for two nights and that proved my point so I stopped. You can understand that, if you research people. It was the time when Walter was still on; I sort of concentrated on Cronkite because he'd abused me. Three Mile Island was the lead crisis; there were about eight crises. Iran was there, the countdown was on, there was an oil crisis, there was a trucker's strike, and there were a couple of others—I think St. Helens was rumbling. There were about eight crises when I watched it one night. And I said, "Dear God, I don't feel bad. After all that, I should be depressed." I felt pretty good. I said, "What's this all about? This is kind of euphoric, almost. This is something abnormal. They must have hidden persuaders in that program." So I decided to watch it the next night carefully and I made notes, and I included the ads. After Three Mile Island—they had Diane Sawyer out there being radiated—they had an ad for Tums, absolutely—Tums. Well, you know, radiation with no acid indigestion. And they had another crisis, and it ran through, and I decided that what they had on was for someone my age that was very reassuring, Tums which is not a problem, but the sort of minor ailments of the aging and the physical indications that you are fading. They had an ad for Polygrip—mint flavored. They went on saying, "Now, it isn't too bad; you can anticipate mint flavor in old age." They had an ad for something that made your false teeth five times whiter. They had an ad—there was a man of about forty chasing a woman about twenty down a beach and he caught her. It wasn't Geritol but it was some kind of tablet. And I said, "Why didn't they give it to her?" The race could go on forever, it seemed to me—you know, a sexist ad. They had an ad for Porcelana which takes the brown spots off your hands. They had one positive ad, I think, in it like Pepsi Cola; and the final ad was ExLax, truly. Two nights in a row they gave the ExLax ad—the only ad I have ever seen for ExLax and they had someone giving it in sign language. They say that the deaf follow Walter Cronkite very closely. Then Walter said, "That's the way it is." And here I was supposed to worry about all these crises for a half hour and Walter wiped it all out, and there it goes, and come back tomorrow night and we'll start over again.

You do that with politics. I don't see how people can make a reasonable judgment on political matter either from political ads or even the news coverage of politics. So you attack the media, it seems to me, and try not to use it, or somehow get around it. I think what Reagan is doing in going to radio is a good idea in terms of how you can communicate politics. You get around the forty-five second projection of it. When you give a television speech, they bring the experts on immediately. Tom Brokaw will tell you what was meant, or you get it filtered through the newspapers. Radio may be the only instrument we have now where you can communicate serious ideas and expect people to listen to it for four or five minutes, if you get them at the right time.

In terms of the actual procedure and the number of proposals around, one has been that you pick delegates by districts. That's been around for a long time. Maine does it, you know. Maine is the only state in the union where you elect the presidential electors by district. It's possible in Maine to have elected three different presidential candidates in any one year. They have two congressional districts and whoever wins in each district gets the delegate, and whoever wins statewide gets two. So theoretically in Maine you could have several candidates and I would say that's better than what we have, better than winner-take-all state procedure. There have been proposals for proportionate allocation of delegates, the sort of thing that was practiced and still is practiced in some of the primaries. Instead of the winner-take-all, if you get 52%, or whoever got 52% will get 52% of the delegates, whoever lost would get 48%. If this is a good principle within the parties, it seems to me it would be a good principle in picking presidential electors, on the grounds that the old justification where the winner-take-all was that the states were so separate and distinguishable from each other that this was a justifiable way to pick electors. For example, in '68 or you can take '72, I think Humphrey got 48% and McGovern got 52% in California and McGovern got the whole delegation. The same thing happened to me and Robert Kennedy. If you say this is a good process within parties, maybe it's a good process in choosing presidential electors.

What I think we should do, and this is simply an extension of the idea of the electoral college, I'd like to see us with about 2500 presidential electoral districts in the country, maybe 100,000 people in each one—about the size of a state senate district, where people would run to be electors. In the New York primary, for example, the candidate is not on the ballot. When I ran there in 1968, the people who were for me had to go around to the voters and say, "My name is Johnson and I'm for McCarthy, you have to find my name on the ballot." Well, if you did that over a period of years you would assume people might get to know who these electors are, the people who run. When the primary was over we had 60% of the delegates to the New York convention, but my name was never on the ballot. They had to go out and canvas house to house and be known and identified. The people had to go to the polls and look for a name and make a choice. The idea would be if we had, say, 2,500 presidential electoral districts in the country where electors would campaign—Republicans, Democrats and Independents—whoever won and you might have to have a run-off, would then go to a national convention. You would have to amend the Constitution because of the state requirement. Have a meeting of these electors and have them decide and pick the President of the United States. A representative process. You could have candidates running with the national hype and all, but you'd still have person-to-person choices within the range of probably 100,000 people which means 50,000 voters. It seems to me you could build a structure of politics and a representative government which would eventually lead to the selection of a President in somewhat the way it was anticipated they would be picked when the idea of the electoral college was established back in 1789.

If you look at the last four or five Presidents I don't know whether one out of five would have been picked through a representative process. Eisenhower wouldn't have been; they'd say, "Look he's just a general, let's pick somebody who knows the issues." I doubt very much that Kennedy would have been picked in 1960. Nixon might have been picked. He was what the Republican party wanted at the time. Jimmy Carter would have been lucky to be a delegate—not to fault him—just in terms of an orderly process of selection. And I don't think Reagan would even have been considered. So if you want a representative process where people who supposedly know more than others make one decision, and another decision, until you move into somewhat like a parliamentary choice of a prime minister, that would be the rational order in which decisions of this kind are made.

It's the way they are made in every corporate structure. You don't have the stockholders run a campaign; let the stockholders pick the president of the company. Yet in politics the national primary idea is that even the limited sort of representative process that goes on now should be set aside and just do it on some kind of broad appeal. More and more people who know to make the decision. And after you have done it, you start to find out what you have elected.

In 1948, that was the last time we had a party platform and we picked Truman and he carried the platform. Since that time you pick a candidate and he tells you what the platform is, and you don't quite know what it is until they make their speeches. McGovern's $1,000 rebate was nowhere in any Democratic platform but he announced it because it was part of his platform. Much of the Carter stuff was never in the platform. I guess Reagan's was not in the platform but he had been talking about it for twenty years so you knew, even before he did anything, he'd do it, but that's how it is.

Well, that's about where we are now. I don't know how this

fits into what you serious people have talked about here in the last year or two, but I think we have to work back to making the process more representative. It is sort of a challenge to the idea that if you have more and more people participate knowing less and less about a subject, especially a candidate, they'll come up with the right decision. As good a proposition as that is to say, "Let's just do it by lot." Run your computers and I think you'll probably come out a little better.

PUTTING THE PARTY AS WELL AS THE PEOPLE BACK IN PRESIDENT PICKING

by
Thomas E. Cronin
and
Robert D. Loevy**

Our nomination process has changed dramatically since the 1960s when John F. Kennedy had to enter just four contested state primaries. Once shaped mainly by state and national party leaders, it is now as much or even more shaped by single-interest groups and the media.

The formal nominating process begins with the Iowa caucus in January of each election year and lumbers through more state caucuses and conventions and thirty-six primary elections before candidates are finally selected at national party conventions in July and August.

Nobody, with the possible exception of Ronald Reagan, seems happy with the present nominating system—especially the patchworky maze of presidential primaries. The process strains the patience of most Americans. Isn't there a better way, ask most Americans, to test a candidate's mind and integrity and encourage quality voter participation?

Critics say the main thing primaries do is eliminate good candidates. The late Adlai Stevenson, a three-time presidential

**About the authors: Tom Cronin, a Democrat, and Bob Loevy, a Republican; both teach political science at Colorado College. Cronin, author of several books including _The State of the Presidency,_ has served this year as a member of the Democratic Party's Commission on Presidential Nominations. Loevy, a former aide to a Republican U.S. Senator, writes frequently for _The Baltimore Sun._ Cronin has been a candidate for Congress.

candidate said the primary system is "a very, very questionable method of selecting presidential candidates. . . . All it does is destroy some candidates." Walter F. Mondale, a few years ago, wrote, "I am convinced . . . that the system itself is becoming increasingly irrational, self-defeating and destructive of the ultimate goal of electing the most important political leader in a free society in the world." Last election season, friends and supporters of Senator Howard Baker (R-Tn.) came away thinking the New Hampshire primary was an unfair as well as unreal test of their candidate's promise as a national leader.

The current primary system plainly favors well-heeled out-of-office individuals who can spend full-time campaigning in selected early state nominating battles. Thus Carter, in 1976, and Reagan, in 1980, could spend up to a hundred days in Iowa, New Hampshire and Florida while the office holders such as Udall, Baker, Anderson, Kennedy and Presidents Ford and Carter had to remain on their jobs as legislators and executives in service to the nation.

Our present nominating process has become a televised horse-race focusing more on rival media consultants and advertising executives than on the competing ideas, programs or even character of the candidates. More voters, to be sure, take part in primary elections than in caucuses and conventions. But what about the *quality* of that participation? Primary voters often know little about the many candidates listed on the ballot. They may drop in at the primary election booth between a trip to the drugstore and the local supermarket and give little more thought to choosing candidates than to choosing among brands of toothpaste and canned vegetables. Popularity polls, slick spot ads, and television coverage of the early primaries offer episodes and spectacles, and the average citizen is hard pressed to distinguish significance from entertainment.

"Winners"—sometimes with only twenty percent of the vote—in the early small state nomination contests are given significant and undue media coverage—and this fact becomes an important part of any savvy campaign strategy. Jimmy Carter's victories in Iowa and New Hampshire in 1976 and the outpouring of cover and feature human interest stories on him are a prime example of this momentum fever.

Voters in New Hampshire and a few other early primaries often virtually get the right to nominate their party's candidate. Candidates who do not do well in these early stages get discouraged and their financial contributors and volunteers

50

desert them. In practice, voters in later states often get presented with just one or possibly one and a half surviving candidates—which leaves many voters in California or Colorado feeling that they have been both cheated and disenfranchised. The final result is that, in most presidential years, the nominees of both major parties are decided much too early in the process.

Critics of the present nominating practices are also concerned, rightly we believe, about the declining importance of the Democratic and Republican National Conventions. Now that nominations are often "sewed up" by winning early primaries, the national conventions have become *ratifying* rather than *nominating* conventions. Most delegates, "bound" by various state and party election rules to vote for a specific candidate, are no longer expected or able to negotiate, bargain and compromise the various diverse interests within the party and work toward nominating a candidate with broad party support. Instead of having real work to do, most delegates have little more to do than cast their predetermined required vote, enjoy a round of cocktail parties, pick up local souvenirs, and then go home. It's all pretty empty and a bit of a charade and it is little wonder that the networks are moving away from gavel to gavel coverage.

A further complaint is that the current nominating system has diminished the role of party and public officials, and concomitantly increased the role of candidate-loyalists and issue activities. Primaries bypass the local party structure. They encourage the candidates and their managers to form candidate-loyalist brigades to support their candidacy several months in advance of the primaries. Elected officials generally are unwilling to become committed to one candidate or another until well along in the election year and hence they are often, in effect, frozen out of the present process. But does this make sense? Hardly. Because most serious candidates for national office hold elective office, or did so in the recent past, the views of their peers who have served with them in Congress or the National Governor's Association can be particularly insightful. Congressman Gillis Long (D-Louisiana) says the rise of primaries and the requirement that delegates be "bound" to a candidate has had the effect of excluding many of the elected officials who in the past would have participated in the nomination of their party's nominee. "We have paid a terrible price for that," Long says. "Most elected officials are attuned to mainstream concerns. For the health and vigor of our party, they need to be involved in the party process. They know the political waters. They know the shoals, and prevailing currents." Because elected officials, especially members of Congress, have some obligation to implement the goals and platform of their party, they should participate in the development of party positions.

The plea from elected officials is as follows: Bring us back into the system; give us incentives for involvement; give us responsibility in selecting our candidates and writing our platform. Let us integrate the national presidential party and the congressional party as one working unit where the various components have some status and voice in the processes and outcomes of the other components.

Those who want to strengthen the party role in the nominating process do not think elected or party leaders should dominate or control nominations. Rather they want to encourage peer review and insure that a reasonable number of elected officials are allowed to participate in the single most significant activity performed by a national party. Political scientist Everett Ladd suggests that the person who successfully "passes muster in a peer review process, if elected, comes into office with contacts and alliances that he needs if he is to govern successfully."

U.S. Senator Alan Cranston (D-Calif.) raises yet another objection to the present system when he says few if any of the qualities that bring victory in primaries are the qualities the presidency demands of its occupants. Cranston may overstate the case, but here is how he thinks:

> Primaries do not tell us how well a candidate will delegate authority. Nor do they demonstrate his ability to choose the best people for top government posts . . . Primaries don't tell us how effective a candidate will be in dealing with Congress, nor how capable a candidate will be at moving the national power structure, nor how good an educator of the American public a candidate would really be as President. And, most important, primaries don't tell us how good a candidate would be at Presidential decision-making. Primaries do not adequately test courage and wisdom in decision-making—yet those are the ultimate tests of a good President.

What follows is a proposal for a pre-primary convention system at the national level—or a national pre-primary convention plan. Our proposal is a recombination of certain state practices fused with some contending "reform" or "rereform" suggestions.

We are more than a little aware that no procedure is neutral, that any system has various side-effects and unanticipated consequences. Further we know that no method of nominating presidential candidates guarantees good candidates or good presidents. (The nominating method used in selecting Lincoln also gave us Buchanan. The nominating method that nominated Eisenhower and Kennedy nominated Richard Nixon as a member of the national ticket on five different occasions.) Plainly, no procedure can substitute for rigorous screening and the exercise of shrewd judgment at every step of whatever system is used.

Still, we want to suggest what we think is a bold, comprehensive and novel better way to select presidential nominees. We offer it as an antidote to the tinkering that characterizes most of the conventional remedies currently being suggested. This is not to say we disagree with many of the suggested incremental changes usually proposed. Rather we think a fresh approach might be even better. We trust it will provoke readers to rethink the existing process and to join the national dialogue on this subject.

The national preprimary convention system would reverse the present order of things. It would replace the present glut of thirty-six individual state primaries with a caucus and convention system in all states, to be followed by a national convention, which in turn would be followed by a national Republican presidential primary and a national Democratic presidential primary to be held on the same day in September. The sequences would look something like this (with illustrative dates):

1. May 1st—Local Precinct Caucuses Throughout the Nation
2. May 14th—County Convention Day Nationwide
3. May 21st—Congressional District Caucuses Nationwide.
4. June 1st—State Conventions Nationwide.
5. July—National Conventions
6. Sept 10th—National Primary Day

Although this proposal runs counter to the present established thinking that the presidential primary should occur before the convention rather than after it, there are working precedents at the state level. The State of Colorado, for example, holds Democratic and Republican party precinct caucuses in early May, in which any registered party member may attend and vote. These precinct caucuses elect delegates to county conventions held in early June, and the county conventions in turn elect delegates to the state party convention, held in early July.

At the state party convention in Colorado, any candidate for statewide office who receives twenty percent or more of the delegate vote is automatically placed on the ballot in the early September primary election. The candidate who gets the highest number of votes is listed first on the ballot, the candidate who gets the second highest number of votes is listed second, and so on down the line. Candidates work hard at the state convention to receive the so-called "top line" designation, and convention delegates have real work to do in deciding who will be on the primary ballot and in what order their names will appear. In the September primary election, the plurality winner receives the party nomination and runs against the opposition party candidate at the regular general election in November.

A few other states have preprimary caucus and convention systems similar to Colorado's, among them Connecticut, Utah, and New York. The proposal thus is new and innovative only when applied at the national level. At the state level, it has been well-tested. Colorado, for example, has used this system since 1910 and has found it to be a good system for retaining the strengths of both the party convention and the party primary election.

A national preprimary-convention plan starts with party caucuses nationwide on the first Monday in May of the presidential year. Any citizen would be eligible to attend a particular party caucus, but all those who vote at the party caucus would have to first register at the caucus as members of that political party. By national law, those who register in a political party at the precinct caucus would be allowed to vote only in that particular party's national primary the following September.

Party members at the party caucus would be eligible to run for delegate to the county party convention. Those candidates for delegate who wished to identify themselves as supporting a particular candidate for President could do so, and they would be bound to vote for that candidate when they attended the county convention.

The county convention would be held on county convention

day on the second Saturday in May. County convention delegates would elect delegates to the state party convention, which would be held on state convention day on the first Saturday in June. The state convention would elect the state delegation to the national party conventions, which would be held in July.

Similar to the procedure at the precinct caucuses, candidates for delegate at the county and congressional district conventions would state their preferences among competing presidential candidates or state their preferences to remain uncommitted at this time. Those stating a preference would then be committed or "bound" on the first ballot at the national conventions. After the first ballot at the national conventions, however, these delegates could exercise their personal judgment in voting for the remaining candidates of their choice.

We propose, and the national preprimary convention plan would readily accommodate, the selection at the state party convention of twenty-five percent of the state's delegation to the national convention as unbound delegates. These persons so designated might be nominated by the state central committees from available state elected and party leaders who have demonstrated strong commitment to their party. Such officials might include several members of the state's congressional delegation, statewide elected officers such as governor and attorney-general, a few big city mayors and state legislators as well as state party leaders. These unbound delegates would sometimes mirror local and state caucus results. But they would have an obligation to exercise their best political judgment, not simply to abide by public opinion and the temporary wishes of their supporters. Their presence and their perspective should help make national conventions more deliberative and more an occasion for party renewal than has been the case in recent years. These officials could also take into consideration late breaking events or reflect current opinion in July as opposed to the public moods earlier in the spring.

It is important to note what would not be allowed in the process outlined here. States would be prohibited by national law from holding any form of official pre-convention presidential primary election. Throughout the entire process, the emphasis would be on selecting party members as delegates. Less than seventy-five percent of the state's delegation will be bound to specified candidates in advance of the convention.

Voting procedures and other operational details at the party caucus, the county convention, congressional districts, and the state conventions would be left to individual state laws and national political party rules. The structure, organization, and scheduling of the Democratic and Republican national conventions would be the same as they are now, with the exception that both conventions would be held in July instead of one convention in July and the other in August.

The major task, as always, of the national convention would be to nominate candidates for the national party primary the following September. There would be two ballots. On the first ballot bound delegates would vote for their declared choice, and unbound delegates could vote for any candidate. After the first ballot, all candidates except for the top three finishers would be eliminated. The top three candidates would then run off against each other on the second ballot, at which time *all* delegates would be unbound and could vote their individual preference.

The authors are of two minds as to what should happen at this point. One of us believes that only the top two remaining candidates (so long as each receives a minimum of thirty percent from the convention) should be placed on the national primary ballot.

The other believes the threshold endorsement should be lowered to twenty-five percent with the possibility that three candidates be allowed on the national primary ballot. If three candidates are placed on the primary ballot, a procedure called "approval voting" would come into effect. Under approval voting, voters can vote for as many candidates as they like. Thus if Reagan, Bush and Baker were on the national Republican primary ballot in September 1984, a moderate Republican might vote for both Baker and Bush, while a conservative Republican might decide to vote for Reagan, or to vote for both Bush and Reagan. Approval voting is, in part, an insurance plan preventing an unrepresentative or least preferred candidate from winning in a three person race. Two centrists can sometimes split the centrist vote between them only to find they both lose to a candidate decidely on the right who wins thirty-five percent of the vote to their combined sixty-five percent (as happened in somewhat similar circumstances when James Buckley won in a New York Senate race in the early 1970s, or as George "Your Home Is Your Castle"

Mahoney did in a Maryland Democratic primary for governor back in the mid-1960s).

Regardless of which formula is used to get two or three candidates on the party's national primary, only those candidates among the top three who received twenty-five percent of the vote or more on the second ballot would appear on the September primary ballot.

On the first ballot, a number of delegates will have voted for candidates who did not finish in the top three. On the second ballot, these delegates will have the opportunity to vote their preference for the party nominee front-runners. The system thus allows delegates to vote their first choices, no matter how weak, on the first ballot, but it also allows all the delegates to participate in the final ranking of the strongest party candidates on the second ballot.

In certain presidential years, a candidate may be so strong at the convention that he will not have to face a national primary election. This will occur when, on the second ballot, one candidate is so strong that neither the second-place candidate or the third-place candidate has twenty-five percent of the convention vote (or under our other alternative, when the second of two top finishers has less than thirty percent). Some states which use the pre-primary convention plan also declare that a candidate who receives seventy percent of the state convention automatically receives the party's nomination, and thus a primary is not needed. This same stipulation would also sensibily apply at the national level. It would be expected, for instance, that a popular incumbent president with strong support within his own party could avoid the strain of a September primary.

The final duty of the national party convention would be to create a pool of acceptable vice-presidential prospects from which the eventual presidential nominee could make a final choice following the national primary in September. All of the candidates who qualify for the second ballot at the convention would automatically be in this vice-presidential pool (although one of them would eventually be removed by winning the party's presidential nomination). The convention could add up to three more vice-presidential candidates to the pool. Immediately following the party presidential primary election in September, the winning candidate would select his vice-presidential nominee from the candidates in the pool. The presidential nominee thus would make the final selection of his vice-presidential running mate, but all the vice-presidential eligibles in the pool would have received "party approval" at the national convention.

The National Democratic Presidential Primary and the National Republican Presidential Primary would both be held on the same day, the second Tuesday after the first Monday in September. This date is suggested because all voters will have returned from August vacations and will have had one week to recover from Labor Day, the three-day holiday annually scheduled for the first Monday in September.

Any voter who was registered in a particular party by July 1 of the presidential year would be eligible to vote in that particular party's national presidential primary election. The date of July 1 is suggested because it is late enough that those citizens who have had their partisan interests stimulated by the local precinct caucuses, the May county conventions, and the June state conventions, still will be able to register in a particular political party. The first of July is early enough to prevent partisan voters from switching from one party to the other after they see which candidates are going to be nominated or which parties are going to have national primaries. The goal here is to prevent partisan voters whose party is not having a presidential primary in a particular year from switching their registration in order to vote for the weakest opposition candidate.

If there are, or should be in the future, any states that do not provide under state law for voter registration in the two major political parties, the United States Congress should pass any necessary national laws to guarantee that all United States citizens have the right to register in a particular political party and vote in the September presidential primary.

The one candidate who gets the most votes in the September primary will be the party candidate in the November general election. A plurality of votes rather than a majority will be sufficient to declare the winner. In case of an exact tie vote, or in case of a close race where large numbers of ballots were contested, or if the winning candidate dies or becomes functionally disabled, the party national committee shall decide the official party candidate for the November election. National law passed by Congress would provide for the details of these procedures.

As noted above, the first official event following the national primary would be the selection of the vice-presidential candidate by the presidential nominee. Notice that the presidential candidate will have considerable latitude in selecting his party running mate. If it appears propitious to select one of his defeated opponents and thereby mend party fences, he is free to do so. If he wishes not to choose a defeated opponent, however, he has three candidates available (one or two of whom he might have pushed for the post) who have been officially approved by the convention.

Some Advantages of the Preprimary Convention Plan

The National Preprimary Convention Plan is designed to eliminate the more criticized characteristics of the present presidential nominating system and also to provide some positive additions not found in the present system:

1. This plan would eliminate the present series of thirty-six individual state primary elections which are so exhausting to the candidates and, eventually, boring to both the news reporters and the average voter. These thirty-six state primaries would be replaced by a single national primary election campaign that would last only six to eight weeks — from the end of the party national convention in July until the early September presidential primary election.

2. The present series of thirty-six individual state primary elections is sometimes unrepresentative of true voter sentiment because turnouts for presidential primaries are relatively low, averaging around thirty percent of registered party voters. The tremendous national interest that would be created by a single national party primary election, held in every state on the same day of the year, would increase voter interest and, accordingly, voter turnout. Turnouts for national presidential primaries often might exceed fifty percent of registered party voters.

3. The present system of thirty-six individual state primaries creates a situation in which candidates who win early primary elections in small and often "unrepresentative" states enjoy a tremendous media advantage in succeeding primary elections. Instead of being noticed because of their personal characteristics or their issue positions, candidates are evaluated mainly on the basis of how they did in previous primaries and how they are likely to do in future primaries. Political "momentum," not character and issues, becomes the main focus of the present pre-convention campaign. The National Preprimary Convention Plan would eliminate this problem of early primaries in

small states being so important relative to later primaries in large states.

4. The present thirty-six state primary system creates artificial regional advantages for those candidates who are lucky enough to have strong support in states that just happen to have early primary elections. The current process which begins in New England and gradually moves south and then elsewhere also minimizes the importance of certain regions such as the Rocky Mountain west and as a result minimizes the need for presidential candidates to respond to the problems of certain regions. The National Preprimary Convention Plan would eliminate these regional advantages by having all Americans in all regions of the country vote in a single national primary on a single day.

5. The present primary election system has reduced the national party conventions to the status of "ratifying conventions" rather than deliberative "nominating conventions." The National Preprimary Convention Plan would revitalize the national convention and give the delegates to the convention real work to do. On the first ballot, the convention delegates will make the first cut in narrowing the field of party presidential hopefuls. On the second ballot, they will determine who will get into the national presidential primary and the order in which the candidates' names will appear on the ballot. As the field of potential winners progressively narrows, from the first ballot to the second ballot, delegates who were bound to first ballot losers will be able to switch their votes away from early losers and to make choices among the finalists. There will also be the issue of the order in which the final nominees are going to finish and the responsible task of creating a qualified and politically-appealing pool of vice-presidential candidates. The dull and boring party national conventions that currently exist will once again become true nominating conventions at which delegates are significant and are lobbied by the various candidates, and have important and challenging decisions to make.

6. The current presidential primary system de-emphasizes the importance of political party membership and the influence of party caucuses and party conventions. Would-be presidential nominees bypass the official party structure by filing directly in preferential primaries and going straight to the voters with techniques such as direct mail, telephone canvassing, and radio and television advertising. In many cases, candidates use hastily-assembled organizations of outside vol-

unteers to defeat the established party hierarchy in the presidential primary.

The National Preprimary Convention Plan would help to restore the importance of the official political party structure while at the same time strengthening the average voter's role in the final decision. In the first stage of the nominating process, candidates would have to make their main appeal to the party activists who are most likely to attend party caucuses and get elected to county conventions and state conventions. People who had not previously considered participating in local party activities might begin doing so in order to be able to advance their preferred presidential candidates. Also increasing the importance of party caucuses and county and state conventions would be the fact that these events would be scheduled on the same day throughout the entire nation.

The broader party electorate would not be side-stepped completely, however. After the party activists have made the first cut at the state level and the national convention has further refined the field, the national party membership will make the final decision in the national presidential primary election.

7. Another problem with holding thirty-six presidential primaries at differing times in thirty-six different states is the fact that the main focus tends to be on local issues in the individual states rather than on national issues of concern to the American people as a whole. This local and state emphasis would continue to exist under the National Preprimary Convention Plan, but only prior to the national convention. After the national convention had limited the field to two or three finalists, these top finishers would have to campaign nationally before the national party electorate in order to win the national presidential primary. National issues would thus often take precedence over local state issues from the time of the convention to national presidential primary day.

8. The current presidential primary system is often criticized for having made contemporary presidents very independent of their own political party organizations. Since the incumbent president's renomination is mainly dependent on support in popular primaries rather than support from party regulars, so the argument goes, the president no longer cares much whether his own party professionals are behind him or not.

The National Preprimary Convention Plan would increase the incumbent president's responsibility to his own political party without reducing the influence of the average party primary election voter. Every incumbent president will want to win "top-line" designation for the primary by finishing first in the second ballot at the national convention. In order to do this, the president will want to cultivate the support of the party activists. Most presidents will thus become more responsible to their own parties.

9. The current thirty-six primary system has been characterized as being unduly influenced by television. Candidates aim their main appeals, so the argument goes, not directly at the voters but at the television cameras through which the vast majority of political information is now filtered to the voters.

Rather than denying the rise of television-politics, the National Preprimary Convention Plan accepts this reality and endeavors to enhance the television-voter relationship. One of the reasons for holding all the party caucuses in the nation on the same day is to make the party caucuses a "super" event that will be thoroughly covered by the news media and thus impart a maximum of political information to the voters. The same thinking applies to the scheduling of a single day for county conventions and a single day for state conventions. The hope is that the tremendous increase in television and other media coverage of the presidential nominating process will result in significantly increased amounts of citizen participation in the nominating process, particularly in terms of increased voter turnouts for the national presidential primaries.

Possible Objections

No plan is perfect and there are some possible defects to the national preprimary convention system. Here are some likely concerns and our discussions of them:

1. The present system has one arguably positive feature that would be less present under the national preprimary convention system. The present series of state primaries that begins with a few smaller states gives lesser known but qualified challengers a chance to make themselves known, and pick up steam (and money) as they move on to some of the larger states. Having all the local caucuses and state conventions taking place at the same time will make it more difficult for less known and less well-financed candidates.

We acknowledge that lesser known candidates will have a somewhat more difficult time under our plan. On the other hand, the cost of entering caucus states is significantly, perhaps five times, less than entering primary states as a serious candidate. Second, a candidate need only do well in a handful of states to prove his or her abilities and capture at least some national attention. Since the nomination will not usually be decided on the first ballot, a number of worthy candidates will be able to survive and thus obtain peer review and political scrutiny before the convention makes its final determination.

2. Some will contend that the national preprimary convention system is too national, too rigid and too mechanistic. They might add that it diminishes federalism, at least to the extent it tells states when and how they will select delegates.

Our response is that the presidency is a national office. Further, it is clear that the national parties have both the responsibility and the authority to decide on the procedure for the nomination of the President. Finally, this new plan will strengthen the party at the state level and it treats all states as equals. No advantage will be given to those living in a particular state just because their state has an early primary or caucus.

3. Critics are likely to say that the national primary feature of this new plan will encourage television and media events of the worst possible kind.

Our response is that our plan will actually diminish much of the negative influence of television in the first and crucial phase of the nominating process — the preconvention stage. It will require presidential candidates to meet with party and elected local leaders and to build coalitions at the grass roots level — not just appear on television spot ads. After the convention, the endorsed candidates will have to rely heavily on television. They will have to appear in debates, or on talk shows, or in addresses to the nation. This is as it should be, for presidents can no longer govern unless they are effective users of electronic media. Thus our plan requires party renewal and party coalition-building skills as well as effective media campaigning.

4. Some critics may fear this will diminish the role of minorities and lessen the affirmative action gains of the past decade — especially gains made in the Democratic party.

We do not think there is evidence that this will be the case. Existing affirmative action rules may just as easily apply. Indeed, the increased turnout at the national primaries should enhance minority participation. And surely this will allow for substantially more minority input than is gained by leaving this crucial decision to the people in a few small unrepresentative states such as New Hampshire.

5. What about its impact on third or minor parties?

Third parties would still have their national conventions. But they would seldom have a need for a national primary. Perhaps some rule could be worked out so that any national party receiving at least five percent in the last presidential election could participate in the national primary arrangements — if they wished to do so.

6. Wouldn't the national primary be an even greater expense to the states?

Perhaps. But nowadays we are already conducting thirty-six primaries and these include most of our bigger states. Conducting the national primary in fifty states in the fall as opposed to thirty-six in the spring is not really much of a difference.

Doubtless there will be additional objections. Our purpose here is not to solve all the technical problems or anticipate all the political side effects. We want to present an alternative that has thus far been overlooked.

Here is a plan, we think, that shortens the formal election season and simplifies it so the average voter can understand its operations. More than the present system, it will test the political coalition-building skills of serious candidates, those skills so needed to win the general election and to govern. More than the present system, it allows for sensible participation from all segments of the party. More than the existing system, it would promote responsible parties that at the same time are subject to popular control. More than the existing system, it would facilitate and encourage the best possible candidates, including busy office-holders, to run for the presidency. And more than the existing system, it would facilitate and encourage thoughtful participatory caucuses and conventions at all levels of our system, and it would go a long way toward rescuing the all but doomed national conventions and help make them more of an occasion for reflective societal leadership.

PART THREE

CONTROVERSIES
and
CONCLUSIONS

CANDIDATES, COALITIONS, INSTITUTIONS and REFORMS

Austin Ranney

MR. THOMPSON: It's a pleasure to welcome you on behalf of the Miller Center to a Gund lecture on the presidential nominating process.

Burkett Miller, whose gift made possible the establishment of the Miller Center, specified in his deed of gift that the Center should, in pursuit of its study and its concentration on the presidency, both seek to enhance a deeper understanding of the presidency and also, in whatever way it could, contribute to improvements in the workings of the presidency. We have undertaken to meet this second objective through national commissions, the most recent being a national commission on the nominating process co-chaired by Melvin Laird and by Adlai Stevenson, III. A key member — the scholar member of the executive board of that commission — is our speaker today. Professor Austin Ranney is past president of the American Political Science Association, professor of political science at the University of Wisconsin and other universities, currently resident scholar at the American Enterprise Institute, the author of numerous books on participation in the nominating process, on party factions, and on the whole gamut of the political process. His distinction for the subject of this evening is that he was a participant in the 1968 reforms which led to certain changes which had both intended and unintended consequences. Not surprisingly, therefore, as seems always to be the case in the social and political arena, another group, fortunately including Professor Ranney, some decade or more later looked again at the nominating process. The results of their deliberation are contained in the Miller Center report.

It is a great pleasure and honor to welcome a friend of many of us and a prominent leader in his field, Professor Austin Ranney.

MR. RANNEY: Thank you very much, Ken. As I am sure many of you know, shortly after he became President, the late John F. Kennedy invited all American winners of the Nobel Prize to a dinner at the White House. When it came time to give the first toast he said that it was the most distinguished gathering of talent and brains and achievement in the White House since Thomas Jefferson had dined alone there. Speaking in his historic hall is an honor and a privilege for which I have no adequate words. I would say beyond this, however, that it is also a great privilege and honor to speak under the auspices of the White Burkett Miller Center, which I think it fair to say is now the most eminent of all of the centers of the study of that key institution of our governmental system, the presidency. Great work had already been done under the leadership of the Center by Professors Ken Thompson and Jim Young. Even greater work lies ahead, and I think that the University of Virginia community can be proud not only of this historic circumstance at your great University but also of the great contributions which the Miller Center has already made and of the many more contributions which it surely will make in the future.

Now, as to the presidential nominating process, political scientists usually describe the form of government of the United States as a presidential democracy. By that they mean a system in which the head of government is a president directly elected by the people and not a prime minister indirectly selected by a parliament. But most political scientists would also go beyond this. They would say that the presidency is the key element in our whole system of government, and that the system works well only when the presidency is working well. Many would also say that the presidency has not been working very well for at least twenty years now, not since Dwight Eisenhower, the last President to serve two full terms of office and the last President to be generally regarded as successful. John Kennedy was assassinated before he could do very much, either good or bad. Lyndon Johnson was driven from office for his identification with an unpopular war. Richard Nixon resigned to avoid almost certain impeachment. Gerald Ford became the first incumbent since Herbert Hoover to be defeated for reelection, and Jimmy Carter became the second. And as I speak tonight the polls show that Ronald Reagan has even less popular approval for his handling of the presidency than any of his predecessors have had at comparable stages in their first two years.

Now, this discouraging record has led many people to ask why our presidents, on whom we depend for so much, seem to do so badly, regardless of whether they are Republicans or Democrats, conservatives or liberals. It is surely one of the most critical questions we face as we approach the 200th anniversary of our constitution. It is being investigated by many of our most skilled and dedicated analysts, some of the most distinguished of whom, as I have already said, are hard at work right here at the Miller Center at the University of Virginia. And it is of course a question with a multitude of aspects, far too many even to be listed in these brief remarks. I therefore propose to focus on just one aspect, namely, the presidential nominating process. I do so without apology, however, for I believe that the kind of people we select to be our presidents has a great deal to do with how well or badly the office works. Not everything, of course, but a great deal. And I also believe that the nominating process by which we choose our major parties' nominees is more important in deciding who will occupy the office in November than deciding whether it will be the Democrat or the Republican. To be concrete, it seems to me that in 1980 the process by which the Republicans settled on Ronald Reagan rather than John Anderson, Howard Baker, George Bush, John Connally, Philip Crane, Robert Dole, or Gerald Ford — plus the process by which the Democrats chose Jimmy Carter rather than Ted Kennedy — eliminated more possibilities and made more important choices than the process by which the voters in November chose Reagan over Carter and Anderson. That is why I shall focus tonight on the presidential nominating process. I propose to ask four questions about it. First, is the process well designed to produce good candidates? Secondly, does the process give those candidates the kind of experience and connections that will help them be effective presidents? Third, does it help to strengthen those other institutions that our nation needs to be governed effectively? And finally, what are the prospects for improving the process?

You all know, a great many people have offered answers to those questions in newspaper columns, television commentaries, political magazines and so on. I think I have read and heard most of what they have said and I find that you can divide the commentators in this question into two big groups. One group seems to have as its motto the old saying, "Virtue is its own reward." Typically these people are quite satisfied with the process. They point out quite correctly that in 1980 about 32 million people participated in selecting the nominees, whereas in every other country in the world only a small handful of party leaders have anything to say about who is going to head the parties. So, these people say, our system is the most democratic in the world, the most open, the best; so it is just fine, leave it alone. To quote a great assistant of another great President, "If it ain't broke, don't mend it."

The other group of commentators on the presidential nominating system seems to have as its motto another old saying, namely, "By their fruits ye shall know them." These people tend to ask not so much is the system intrinsically fair or participatory or open or democratic; they ask instead, does it produce good results? Does it produce good candidates? Does it give the people good education on the issues? Does it give good preparation for those candidates to become Presidents?

It should be evident from the way I have described both of these groups that I identify myself with the second, and so all of the questions that I intend to deal with tonight are concerned with the results of the process rather than with its intrinsic fairness or the degree of participation in it or whether it makes good entertainment or anything else.

So I turn then to the first question. Is the process well-designed to produce good candidates? Most people, I suppose, have probably answered this question in terms of whether they are enthusiastic about Carter or Reagan or both. And it might be very difficult to find a large number of people that we could analyze, as social scientists like to do, because there is a good deal of evidence that there was a higher level of dissatisfaction with the two major party candidates in 1980 than there has ever been in any previous presidential election since modern public opinion polling first started. The best evidence of this is provided by the Center for Political Studies at the University of Michigan, which has been conducting studies of the presidential electing process going back to 1952. In each of its surveys it has been asking its respondents to rank the presidential candidates on a scale from zero (awful) to one hundred (absolutely perfect). And in 1976 the average ratings given by the voters to the two candidates were by far the lowest they had ever been. They averaged in the low 20s for the two candidates as compared with, for example in the 50s and 60s when Eisenhower was running against Stevenson. There is other evidence as well. A number of the states in the 1980 primary elections had on their ballots a "none of the above" line where you could vote for Carter or Kennedy or for "none of the above." And there were actually two states in which "none of the above" finished second — the first time in history in which that has happened.

I recognize that many people, when they hear evidence of this sort, will say, well yes, but after all under the earlier system there were a lot of pretty poor candidates, too. After all, look at Harding and Coolidge (and I think I could say, especially in the heart of Virginia, look at Grant). They certainly were poor nominees and poor presidents, so there is merit to that argument. I would add that there is no system that is guaranteed always to produce good candidates nor is there any system that is always guaranteed to produce bad candidates. In moments of nostalgic longing when I am asked what system do you really favor, Mr. Ranney?, I sometimes say that I favor the congressional caucus system, which produced such candidates as Thomas Jefferson and James Madison and James Monroe, and then we got rid of it because it wasn't democratic and participatory enough. Then they say, seriously now, what kind of system, do you favor? I think the answer to that has to be that it is beyond the human mind to produce a system guaranteed always to produce great candidates and, equally, there is no way of producing the system that is guaranteed always to produce bad candidates. It seems to me the question is properly asked, rather, are there particular systems that tend to favor certain kinds of candidates rather than other kinds of candidates?, and I would say that the real test of any system is the kind of candidates it produces *most* of the time.

In trying to answer that question it seems to me that we have to recognize that certain aspects of our current presidential nominating system advantage certain kinds of candidates and disadvantage others. One of the aspects is something that a number of observers have pointed to, including the report of the Miller Center Commission to which Professor Thompson referred. It is the absence of what might be called "peer review." That is to say, the present nominating system provides no regularized process by which the government and party leaders, who know the potential aspirants to the presidency on the basis of having dealt with them in legislatures or in executive positions, have any special say about who is good presidential timber and who is not. The fact is that presidential nominations are made by ordinary voters voting in the primaries. It is also the fact that most of the knowledge that most voters have about the presidential nominees is knowledge they have gained exclusively from the mass media, especially television, and not from any kind of face to face contact.

If I may indulge in a slight aside, I think that that has real consequences about the kind of candidate we have. I am a citizen of Maryland but because the Washington television market is what it is, I followed the recent Virginia gubernatorial campaign as closely as most citizens of Virginia did, at least as far as TV advertising is concerned. And my main difficulty was that I had difficulty remembering as each ad came on which candidate was which, which one was Robb and which one was Coleman, because they seemed to me to be almost indistinguishable. Both were good looking young men, well dressed, rather cool, or, as they say in California, "laid back," and difficult to distinguish from each other. It occurred to me that perhaps we have here the answer to one of the greatest mysteries of presidential politics in 1980 — the mystery of what happed to John Connally. Connally, as you know, refused to accept any federal money for his campaign so that he could spend any amount of money that he could raise and he is said to have spent over eleven million dollars in return for which he got one delegate. If I may paraphrase the late Sir Winston Churchill, never in the history of human politics has so much money been spent by a candidate for so few delegates. Yet when John Connally was speaking to live audiences in auditoriums he was a great stump orator—one of the best in present-day politics. He regularly got cheering, stomping, whistling ovations from live audiences. He entered a number of primaries, spending most of his money, as candidates do these days, on television campaigns, and he was a terrible failure. Why? I am not a total believer in all of the works of Marshall McLuhan, but I do believe in his famous insight that the television is a "cool" medium, whereas others — for example, stump speaking—are "hot" media. And the kind of politician who comes across well through the flickering light of the tube in people's living rooms is a very different kind of politician than one who comes across well through the hot medium of speaking to two or three thousand people in an auditorium. In my opinion, that is the main thing that happened to John Connally: he is a hot personality, he campaigned largely on the cool medium of television, and as a result he failed miserably.

Much the same case could be made about Ted Kennedy, and

my suspicion is that one impact of television on the future of politics is that there are going to be more and more Robbs and Colemans doing well, and fewer and fewer Connallys and Lyndon Johnsons and Hubert Humphreys and Ted Kennedys. That may be wrong but it is at least an interesting hypothesis well worth looking at.

In any event it seems to me that it is quite clear that we do not have any peer review and that most of the screening of candidates that goes on, goes on through the electronic media, and that most of the people who select the candidates, the people who vote in the primaries, select on the basis of what they have seen on the tube.

The second characteristic is a characteristic which is being very vividly illustrated now. A number of political scientists were shocked by the fact that Jimmy Carter started all-out campaigning for the 1976 Democratic nomination almost two years before the Democratic convention met. Unprecedented to start that early, they said. It may have been unprecedented then, but in the strictest legal sense of the term, Walter Mondale and Ted Kennedy began campaigning for the 1984 Democratic nomination within a matter of a few weeks after November 1980. Carter's concession speech had hardly ceased tinkling in the ears of the national audience when Mondale and Kennedy started beating the bushes. In fact, the Mondale organization has been registered with the Federal Election Commission (and campaigning and raising money) ever since February of 1981. So in effect, presidential campaigns nowadays never cease.

Why? I think the answer lies in what many commentators call the "front-loading" of the primaries; that is, the fact that what happens in Iowa and New Hampshire at the beginning of the campaign is twenty times more important than what happens in the much bigger states of California and Ohio and New Jersey at the end of the campaign. Hence it is critical for a candidate to do well in the early primaries and caucuses, because if he does well there the media will announce to the world that he is the front runner, the candidate to beat. Given that kind of momentum and given the proportional allocation of delegates in the later primaries the candidate can ride that early momentum to victory as indeed has been the case with all of the winners in recent years.

Now, the kind of politics that enables one to do well in Iowa and New Hampshire is what political scientists call "retail politics." That is, the candidate does not so much appear on the tube and give great speeches to large audiences. Rather, he emphasizes meeting with small groups in coffee clatches and school rooms where there may be no more than twenty or thirty people present and the object is personally to shake the hand of every individual voter. And Mr. Mondale is already very well launched on such a campaign.

Does that favor certain kinds of politicians over others? I think it does, at least in one regard. After he withdrew from the 1980 contest for the Republican nomination, Howard Baker, one of the most effective leaders of either party in Washington, said rather ruefully that he guessed you had to be an unemployed politician to make a serious bid for the presidency. One indeed wonders if it is a coincidence that Mr. Carter and Mr. Reagan were able to campaign fulltime as ex-governors holding no other position when their leading opponents were either incumbent presidents or incumbent senators who had to stay at home in Washington, at least a certain amount of time, and tend to their governmental knitting. It seems to me that in the current contest Mr. Mondale has a considerable advantage, assuming that he has overcome his historic aversion to Holiday Inns. He is able to campaign fulltime, something that his other leading opponents, such as Senator Hart and Senator Glenn, are not able to do. Such a system does not guarantee that outsider candidates are always going to win, but it seems to me undeniable that the system, as it now works, tilts in favor of the outsider.

Although there is no way of proving it, I think that Ronald Reagan might well have been nominated under the old system as well as under the new system because, after all, he was a well-known figure in the Republican party and was a well-known national figure and had run for the presidency on two previous occasions, almost winning the presidential nomination in 1976. But it is inconceivable that Jimmy Carter could have been nominated under the old system where only people who were well-known to a large number of the national leaders of their party could hope to win its nomination. Some people will regard the fact that the present nominating system makes it possible for a Jimmy Carter to be nominated as a strong argument in its favor, while others may regard it as a strong argument against the system. I am not going to make either of those arguments. I am simply going to say that, given the frontloading of the primaries, the ability of the outsider to come in and, by early victories, build up a kind of a momentum which, with a boost from the media, will ultimately carry him to the nomination, is possible under the new system in a way in which it was not under the old system. So, deciding whether the system produces better candidates or worse candidates depends on how you feel about Reagan and Carter. But if one asks, does the system make it easier for outsider candidates by giving them advantages that they did not used to have, the answer, it seems to me, is yes.

We turn now to the second question: does the process give the candidates the connections and experiences they need to govern effectively? I have a little story to tell that illustrates my views on that question. It took place in 1977 after the Democratic party's Winograd reform commission had met. The newly-elected President Carter called in the commission for a reception in the White House to thank its members for their labors, and he made a little speech. The basic point of the speech was that the thing of which he was most proud was that he owed his nomination to no organized interest group, but only to the people: the people had given him the nomination in the primaries, the people had elected him over Ford and he felt indebted to nobody other than the people. I remember thinking at the time, well, Mr. President, I hope that when things begin to get difficult for you you will find that 'the people' out there will give you support you need because you will find that the organized groups, the congressmen and the pressure groups and the labor unions, are not going to feel any more indebted to you than you feel to them. This is not the occasion for me to discuss what went well and what went badly in the Carter administration, but it would be fair to say that he got precious little help from those groups, and that made effective governing a lot more difficult for him.

The point is that in the old days before the "reforms" of the 1970s, presidential nominations were won primarily by presidential aspirants and their representatives talking to the powerful governors, mayors, senators, state chairmen and the like. The aspirants got to know those influential people well in that process, and later on, when they became presidents, they had already developed substantial networks of relationships that they were able to use to build up the support they needed to get their programs adopted. Under the present nominating system that is no longer the case. An aspirant does not win the nomination by lining up endorsements of the parties' leaders. Senator Edmund Muskie went that route in 1972, he got the endorsements of almost all of the party's leading members, and it turned out to be worth absolutely nothing when he did not do as well in the New Hampshire primary as the media expected him to do. And George McGovern, who had a few major leaders' endorsements swept to the nomination. Jimmy Carter won the 1976 nomination in the same way, and that was substantially the case with Ronald Reagan in 1980. So, endorsements by party leaders are not only useless, in fact there is a rather substantial advantage, if the truth were known, for running *against* the "party establishment," for making it clear that you are an outsider, a new broom, and have not had any part in that mess in Washington.

In short, we have succeeded in separating the process of building the coalition needed to win a nomination from the process of building the coalition needed to govern. Nominating politics and governing politics are two quite different operations in a way that they never have been in the past. And it just may be that the kind of politician and organization that is best for nominating politics may not be so good for governing politics. History may reverse the judgment, but it is quite common for people now to regard Jimmy Carter as not a very successful president, as politically inept, as ineffective at handling his relations with Congress. What we tend to forget is that, from at least one point of view, Jimmy Carter is one of the greatest politicians in American history. I would argue that Jimmy Carter's feat of winning the Democratic nomination in 1976 as an almost total unknown and outsider is one of the great political feats of history. Then in 1980, even though the early polls showed him running 25 and 30, he won the nomination again — with, to be sure, a little help from the Ayatollah Khomeini. So he was magnificent at nominating politics, and the fact that he could be one of the great nominating politicians in history and one of the least effective governing politicians in history strikes me as a vivid illustration of how much we have separated nominating politics from governing politics. This does not mean that no one who ever wins a presidential nomination is ever again going to be an effective president. It does mean that if that does happen it will be because we are lucky, not because there is anything in the nominating process that produced the kind of people likely to be good at governing.

That leads to my third question: has the presidential selection process strengthened the *institutions* we need to govern effectively? It is well to begin answering this question by remembering that our constitutional system was deliberately and brilliantly designed by the fifty-five men who wrote it *not* to produce effective government capable of taking swift and purposive action. It was designed to make it difficult for government to act at all if it has to against the strong objections of any significant part of the community. Thus, separation of powers; thus, federalism; thus checks and balances and all those other institutions that were designed not to make it easier for government to get good things done but to make it difficult for government to do bad things. Yet, every government on occasion needs some way of focusing its powers so that it can develop and implement effective policies, particularly in emergencies like great depressions or wars. Over the years American government has developed a series of institutions, political parties for one, a strong presidency for another, a powerful bureaucracy for another, as ways under certain conditions of bypassing the built-in centrifugal tendencies, of our governmental system.

How has the new nominating process affected those institutions? Very clearly it has played an important role in weakening our political parties. In fact, I would say that as far as presidential politics is concerned we now have in this country effectively a no-party system. Do not misunderstand me — into the indefinite future a person will have to be labeled either Republican or Democrat to have a serious shot at the Presidency. But the point is that those labels are going to be won by the individual entrepreneurial candidate organizations who win the primaries. The labels certainly are not going to be awarded by groups of party bosses meeting in smoke-filled rooms deciding to whom they will give the honors. Certainly no set of bosses is now meeting or will ever meet to decide that the 1984 Democratic nominee is going to be so-and-so, or, for that matter, the Republican nominee is going to be so-and-so. Political parties used to play important roles in raising money for presidential campaigns. Now they play very minor roles. Political parties and their national chairmen used to be the main organizers of presidential campaigns. Now the campaigns are run by the candidate organizations, and the parties have little voice in strategy or tactics.

As a result, the national political parties have just about disappeared, except as labels, from presidential politics. With regard to the power of the presidency, as a result of the Vietnam war and as a result of the Watergate scandals, the formal powerful bureaucracy. Efforts were made by President Carter to reduce the power of the bureaucracy. Efforts by President Reagan are being made along the same lines and efforts by the next President and the President after him and the President after him will undoubtedly also be made and no doubt that power may even be eroded a bit. But of all of the classical institutions for making up for the weakness of our fundamental political agencies of government, the bureaucracy is the one least changed in recent years.

These, I believe, are some of the consequences of the new presidential nominating process. Some would say that the new process is still an improvement on the old one: it is more open and more democratic and more participatory, and these virtues are their own reward. Others, including me, say that the new process is worse because it is less likely to produce candidates who have the kind of experience and know-how that will make them effective Presidents. It is less likely to give them the kind of experience and the connections that they need in order to be effective Presidents and it has a strong tendency to weaken those institutions of government that any President needs to govern effectively.

My final question is: what are the prospects for improving the process? In recent years, especially since 1980, a number of commentators and organizations have studied the process and have sought ways of improving it. The most notable so far have included the commission headed by former Governor Terry Sanford of North Carolina, the Miller Center Commission co-chaired by Melvin Laird and Adlai Stevenson III, the Democratic party's fourth reform commission chaired by North Carolina's governor James Hunt, and a commission headed by Chancellor Alexander Heard of Vanderbilt University which is going to spend several years studying the problem before it makes its report. The recommendations that have been made by the commentators and the commissions are remarkably similar in their diagnosis of what is wrong with the current presidential nominating process and in their suggestions about what might be done about it. For example, all three commission reports argue strongly that the absence of any element of peer review is a great deficiency in the presidential nominating process and they recommend a variety of measures for restoring some element of it, of which the most notable, made by all three commissions, is that ex-officio, uncommitted official delegate voting slots be given to the parties' elected officials, to the parties' governors, senators, representatives, perhaps mayors, perhaps state party chairs, — in short, to a large number of the people who under the present rules are denied any kind of ex-officio seats.

They also all agree that the delegates ought to be given a chance to make up their own minds. They all strenuously object to Rule 43c that was adopted by the Democrats in their convention in 1980, which required every delegate to vote for the candidate on whose slate he was elected in the primary to support, and provided that if the candidate had any reason to believe that the delegate would not faithfully honor his pledge that candidate had the right to remove that delegate. All three commissions voted for the rescinding of any such rule on the ground that, given the long time between the first and last primaries, the candidate who looked marvelous in the snows of Iowa and New Hampshire in the late winter may look very different in terms of desirability in the heat of New York or Kansas City or Chicago or Philadelphia when it comes time actually to cast their votes in the conventions.

A third conclusion on which all agree is that the financial restrictions that presently which place such a premium upon a candidate's ability to raise money in small contributions — which only candidates who have a very strong ideological following on either the far left or the far right can hope to have — encourage extremists and disadvantage moderates. So all recommend raising the ceilings on campaign contributions by individuals.

The Miller Center Commission report is the only one that so far has directly tackled one of the most difficult of all of the problems: the proliferation of the presidential primaries. It has recommended that the number of primaries be reduced to a maximum of sixteen and that those states that do choose to have primaries must hold them in regional primaries organized by time zones, and that, furthermore, the order in which those primaries are held should be determined by lot rather than one particular time zone always coming first.

What are the prospects that all or some of these reforms will be adopted? Of course the Hunt Commission's reforms have already been adopted. What about the Sanford Commission's suggestions and the Miller Center Commission's suggestions? We can be hopeful, but I do not think we can be confident that, for example, of the present thirty-six states holding primaries enough are going to drop them that we are only going to have sixteen primaries in 1984. In fact, in mid-1982 more states are considering adding presidential primaries than dropping them. It seems to me that the next logical step down the road, one that I would not welcome but that I think is a real possibility, is the adoption of a one day national presidential primary and the complete abolition of the conventions — something that according to the most recent Gallup polls, is favored by seventy percent of the American people.

If adopted, will the reforms help? My feeling is that at the most they can only have a marginal effect. They may, particularly in the Democratic party, have a beneficial effect upon the platform writing process because they will involve in the platform-writing process some of the senators and congressmen and governors who have a real stake in seeing that the platform is something more than what Stuart Eizenstat called the 1980 Democratic platform: "the sum total of the maximum demands of every interest group represented at the convention."

But it seems most unlikely that if a particular candidate has "swept through the primaries" or has been declared by the media as "the clear winner of the primaries," no convention, however unbound by formal pledges and however many party leaders attend it, is going to deny that candidate the nomination. You can just imagine the howl that would go up from the media if that should happen. On those rare occasions where we have closely contested conventions of the Reagan-Ford type in 1976, the new rules might make a difference; but that kind of closely-contested convention will not happen very often.

So I conclude that the new reforms will make, at the most, only marginal improvements in what I have been describing. And if that is the case, it seems to me appropriate to end these remarks with the famous phrase with which the Supreme Court opens each of its sessions: "God save the United States."

CONCLUSION

On one issue, a consensus has emerged in discussions of the presidential nominating process. The present system clearly falls short both of the aims of the founders and the needs of the present era. Neither reforms nor retrenchment in returning to earlier practices offer secure answers to present problems. Yet some observers look well beyond the nominating process to more far-reaching trends and forces. Others say that dissatisfaction with the nominating process is at most a parochial question inspired by the attitudes of partisans of a single political party, the Democrats.

Whatever the opinions and viewpoints expressed in the public arena, recurrent discussions of the need for change justify serious attention to the problem. The main value of a slender volume such as this one bringing together the best thought of respected writers and scholars is the strong light it throws on unsolved problems. On the issues, the authors demonstrate a large measure of unanimity. On the answers, they set forth a broad range of propositions some of which clash with and contradict others. Not surprisingly, some proposals call for far-reaching changes while others reflect skepticism, based on past experience, that reforms will improve or alter circumstances.

Yet the gravamen of the discussion running through the separate papers is a clear recognition we can do better. The test of a policy or a process is its consequences. The measure of the nominating process are the candidates it produces judged against those who fall by the way. If scholars and observers were convinced of the superiority of the former over the latter, the controversies over the workings of the nominating process would be less intense. It is precisely the disappointment that many serious-minded Americans feel at the end result of the process that generates periodic study and review.

We believe that the two contributions of the Miller Center to the understanding and improvement of the nominating process have complementary value and importance. The essays on the nominating process contained in this volume are a worthy addition to scholarly discussion of the problem. They constitute an effort by the Center to bring together the fruits of long and careful research and study by some of the country's best minds addressed to several aspects of the process. The Center is also proud of the report which has been issued by a national commission co-chaired by Melvin Laird and Adlai Stevenson III directed more explicitly to a concerned public and to policymakers. Taken together, this volume and the commission's report constitute a response to the Center's dual mandate to further understanding of the presidency and to contribute to its improvement. We have followed this dual guideline throughout all our activities and programs and intend to continue to do so in two additional volumes on the presidential nominating process now in preparation.

REPORT OF THE COMMISSION ON THE PRESIDENTIAL NOMINATING PROCESS
February 2, 1982

No political process in the United States is more important than our method of nominating presidential candidates, yet none has given rise to so much dissatisfaction. From both ends of the political spectrum come demands for change. A growing resolve on the part of concerned Americans to find a solution to this problem unites Democrats and Republicans, liberals and conservatives, advocates and opponents of recent reforms. This new movement knows no partisan cast nor does it seek to benefit any one candidate or faction. It is motivated solely by the belief that the public interest is ill-served by the current nominating system. Its conviction is as simple as it is significant: reforms there must be and reforms now.

As a result of this interest in reform, the Miller Center created a bipartisan commission to examine every facet of the process by which our two major political parties go about selecting their respective candidates for president. The Commission has collected the views of scores of political leaders and considered the suggestions of numerous scholars, political analysts, and interested citizens. This report summarizes the concerns of these people and expresses the common objectives for reform that underlay their testimony. It then sets forth a set of specific proposals, considered during the testimony, that Commission members believe will best promote these objectives. The changes we advocate are few in number, practical, and capable, for the most part, of being implemented immediately.

Because the responsibility for making changes in the nominating process is currently divided among many different bodies and levels of government, this report addresses several audiences. A reasonably coordinated approach to reform will require action by the Congress, the president, both national parties, the state parties, the governors, and the state legislatures. The willingness of these authorities to act will also be influenced by the number of groups and citizens who join in the movement for reform and urge their representatives and party officials to make the needed changes.

The Nominating Process: Where We Stand Today

The transformation of the nominating process over the last two decades has been both dramatic and profound. As recently as 1960, most delegates to the party conventions were chosen in state party caucuses and possessed the discretion, as representatives, to exercise an independent choice about their party's nominee. Presidential primaries played an important, but secondary, role, and many of the delegates chosen in primaries still retained and exercised their right to make their own decisions. By 1980, only twenty years later, some thirty-seven states held primaries, and nearly three-quarters of the delegates were committed to vote for a particular candidate on the basis of the primary results. The state caucuses—except for Iowa—received little attention; and with the knowledge that the delegates chosen in primaries would be bound in their convention votes, caucuses had little reason or incentive to select uncommitted delegates. For all practical purposes, the outcome of the nominating races was decided by primary voters, not delegates; and the voters, far from being able to express their real choice, often discovered that circumstances created by the scheduling of the primaries reduced their options or rendered their votes meaningless.

Over the same period, the financing of nominating campaigns also drastically changed. In 1968, candidates raised funds on their own with few restrictions as to their source and no restrictions as to the size of the contributions or expenditures. Thus Robert Kennedy, responding to the new political climate created by the New Hampshire primary results in 1968, entered the race in March and in a brief eighty-five day campaign raised nine million dollars. By 1980, only twelve years later, all candidates seeking nomination who accepted public funding faced limitations on how much they could spend both within each state and for the national campaign as a whole. Nearly all official campaign contributions had to be reported; their sources had to be publicly disclosed; and they were subject to limitations of $1000 for an individual contributor and $5000 for a registered political group. (There was no limitation, however, on independent expenditures outside of the official campaign, and for the first time in presidential nominating politics the independent expenditures of nationally based political action committees began to play a significant role, following a pattern recently established in congressional races.)

Taken together these changes dramatically altered the strategic environment of the nominating campaigns and changed the way in which candidates could seek to become their party's presidential candidate. The power of state and local party organizations and of elected party officials also greatly diminished between 1960 and 1980; in their place stand the national party labels which the individual aspirants now seek to capture by strategies of intimate village politics in the first contests (Iowa and New Hampshire) and by mass popular appeals thereafter. New power centers, in particular the national media, have moved into this vacuum and have come to exercise considerable influence over the outcome of the nominating decision. The candidates, obliged to fashion their campaign tactics to suit this new environment, think chiefly in terms of activating certain mass constituencies and pay less attention to negotiating and forging links with party leaders. The knowledge that voters, not delegates, will decide the results, combined with the time-consuming task of raising money in small sums to qualify for public financing, has forced candidates to begin their active campaigns much earlier than before. The media and public follow these developments, extending the active campaign for so long that public interest can give way to public apathy.

Considering these changes with hindsight, it might be imagined that they were part of a single, comprehensive plan to transform the nominating process. In fact, this was not the case. The changes were undertaken by different authorities—national parties, state parties, state governments, and the federal government—acting at different times under differing impulses. Frequently, they were reacting to each other's decisions. Yet as often as not they were misinterpreting each other's intentions or responding to consequences that had been neither desired nor foreseen. So the system we have now is more the result of unintended consequences and mutual miscalculations than deliberate design. Moreover, no one claims responsibility for this system because no one ever wanted it to be as cumbersome, complex, and confusing as it is.

Nor does the nominating process reflect a consensus on the part of party officials or political leaders. In actuality, no two presidential campaigns since 1968 have been conducted under the *same* rules and laws. No sooner has one nominating campaign ended than legislators and party officials have initiated modifications for the next one. The effort to change the nominating process today cannot, therefore, be depicted as a threat to a settled institutional system. On the contrary, it is another —although quite different—step in a continuing search to solve a problem that has vexed American politics for more than a decade.

Many of the recent changes have, of course, represented indisputable improvements. Certain undemocratic abuses in the selection of delegates, offensive to proponents of any legitimate system, have been abolished; groups, notably blacks and women, that in some instances were effectively shut out of participation in the process have been included; and the pall of illegal campaign contributions and excessive financial dependence on a few sources has been lifted.

Yet the system as a whole, despite these improvements, has proven unsatisfactory. In testimony after testimony, the Commission heard the same litany of unstinting criticism: that the active public phase of presidential campaigns is too long, diverting the attention of the public and political leaders from the business of governing the nation; that the democratic appearance of the decision-making process is often specious, with participation low and with many voting after the nomination decision has already been made; that there are too many incentives for candidates to create factional divisions within the parties and not enough to promote consensus; and that the rules of campaign finance produce unnecessary burdens for the candidates and interfere too greatly with the expression of natural political forces.

Many who testified before the Commission commented on their personal observations as participants in the nominating process, comparing their experiences before and after the recent reforms. This information was used to illustrate the problems of the nominating process and to assist in the search for viable reforms in the years ahead. No one proposed past systems as rigid models that should—or could—be reinstituted in their entirety. The tired debate about whether the nominating process before 1968 was superior to that after 1968 played no role whatsoever in the Commission's deliberations.

Principles and Objectives for Reform

The general goals of the nominating process are clear. People want a system that is fair and takes into account the preferences of the party rank and file, including those who do not vote in primaries; a system that selects qualified candidates capable of exercising the responsibilities of the presidency; a system that does not encourage unnecessary divisions within the parties; and finally a system that promotes the delicate network of contacts among political leaders that will enable a president to govern effectively.

These general goals serve as the standards by which people ultimately try to judge and evaluate the performance of the nominating process. They are, however, too far removed from the immediate structure of the nominating process to serve as working principles of reform. In considering the views of all those who testified, the Commission sought to elicit a set of concrete objectives that would promote these goals and at the same time could serve as a practical guide for party officials and legislators. No one claims that it is possible to demonstrate a perfect cause and effect relationship between these concrete objectives and the general goals, but the list the Commission has arrived at represents its best judgment of how the performance of the nominating process could be improved over the long run.

We accordingly urge changes in the rules and laws of the nominating process that will achieve the following four objectives:

1. A mix of delegate selection systems and a scheduling of delegate selection contests that does not serve artificially to reduce options, come to premature decisions, or cut off choice and deliberation in the decision on the presidential nominees.

2. A method of choosing and mandating delegates that leaves enough of them with discretionary judgment such that the choice of the nominee by the delegates is a genuine possibility.

3. A method of selecting delegates that encourages the choice of individuals who are knowledgeable about politics and committed to the long-term interests of their political party.

4. A system of financing nominating campaigns that precludes both the possibility and the appearance of corruption, but which otherwise avoids all unnecessary legal interference in the conduct of campaigns.

Specific Proposals

This list of objectives was supported by the testimony given before the Commission and represents what we believe is a consensus today among the nation's political leaders. Using these objectives as its starting point, and considering all the specific suggestions of those who testified, we have drawn up a list of specific proposals to achieve those objectives. They are presented below within the context of the central aspects of the selection process:

I. The mix of selection systems between primaries and caucuses. One of the most frequently heard complaints was that both parties have too many primaries, placing unnecessary burdens on the candidates and detracting from the deliberative process that should determine the nomination results. Primaries do, of course, serve as *one* valuable method of judging rank-and-file preferences. But a nearly total reliance on primaries not only conflicts with other objectives of the nominating process, but also provides an imperfect and unreliable way of determining the popular will. Primaries by their nature allow voters to express only a first preference, and all second or third preferences, which are necessary for determining majority sentiments in a multi-candidate race, are lost. The primary electorate, moreover, is not always representative of the views of either the party's traditional supporters or the electorate as a whole. Participation in primaries is low and has generally been decreasing, and primary voters tend to be wealthier, more highly educated, and more ideologically motivated than the electorate at large.

There is no question that caucus systems suffer from faults of their own. But in states where the parties are reasonably strong and representative of their popular constituents, caucus methods can be relied on to select competent delegates who are in touch with the basic sentiments of those whom they represent. The recent binding of delegates in caucuses, almost to the same degree as in primaries, should not be seen as the natural tendency of this system; rather, it is the result of the caucuses' secondary role in the entire process and of certain rules, especially in the Democratic party, that have discouraged a discretionary role for the delegates.

In light of these considerations, the Commission recommends the following concrete steps:

1. A reduction in the number of primaries to no more than sixteen.

2. Greater flexibility for state parties in caucus states, with a view to making caucus procedures more attractive. Specifically national party rules should be relaxed to permit states to set aside a certain number of formally uncommitted delegates above and beyond those that emerge as uncommitted from the normal selection process.

II. The selection and mandating of delegates. The delegates and conventions today have lost their discretionary role. No change is more important than to return to the delegates and the conventions the practical possibility of making an independent judgment. Once delegates and conventions possess this authority, it is essential that the delegates themselves have the qualities and qualifications to exercise their authority with wisdom and discretion. The issues of freeing the delegates and ensuring their competence are thus intimately linked, and achieving the former without considering the latter would be a serious mistake.

The objective of returning discretion to the delegates is not a movement against democracy. If delegates are seriously to reflect the public's will in a multi-candidate race, they must take into account not only their constituents' first preference but also their second and third. Beyond that, the choice of the presidential nominee is one in which those who have served their party long and loyally should have a voice. They are, after all, practiced in the art of politics; they have direct personal knowledge of the candidates; and they will continue to work directly with the candidate if he or she is elected, assuring the president of a coalition that will make government work. There is nothing elitist or anti-democratic in according such a measure of discretion to responsible representatives.

To achieve the goals of a deliberative process with knowledgeable delegates, every effort should be made to reduce the number of formally committed delegates and to assure that many of those who are uncommitted possess the *de facto* discretion to exercise an independent judgment. The Commission favors measures designed to include a large share of elected officials and party officers as regular participants at the conventions, to a level of more than twenty percent. Specifically, the Commission recommends the following steps:

1. Changes in state laws and party rules to assure that all delegates, no matter how they are chosen, would retain the op-

tion of exercising independent judgment in their convention vote.

2. The inclusion of *ex officio* delegates—drawn from among members of Congress, governors, and high party officials—who are not bound by the results of state delegate selection contests.

3. The selection in primary states, without enlarging existing delegations, of a percentage of delegates chosen outside the primary process and not bound by its results.

III. The scheduling of delegate selection contests. The current sequential arrangement of primaries tends artificially to narrow the choice of candidates and to reduce the options not only of the delegates but of those who vote in primaries during the latter stages. In addition, it gives an unjustifiable degree of influence to those states (Iowa and New Hampshire) that hold their delegate selection contests well in advance of the others. In 1980, for example, the nomination decision had effectively been made before nearly one-fifth of the population went to the polls to choose their delegates in the June 3rd primaries.

Combined with the above steps to reduce the number of primaries and to include more uncommitted delegates, changes in the scheduling of primaries would help to reduce the undesirable effects of the current arrangement. The objective is not to eliminate completely the existence of a sequence, for the sequence has the positive effects of allowing lesser known candidates a reasonable chance and permitting the people and delegates to observe the candidates over a series of different contests. These benefits can, however, be maintained without creating the extensive problems of the current schedule.

In light of these considerations, the Commission recommends the following measures:

1. The national parties should enforce a strict time frame within which primaries, caucuses, and "beauty contests" or straw polls may be held, beginning no earlier than the first week in March and ending no later than the first week in June.

2. For those states that do choose to hold primaries, the national parties or Congress should fix regional primary dates within this period, defining the regions according to time zones. For each election year the order of these primaries would be established by lottery.

IV. Campaign financing. The most important objective of campaign finance rules is to avoid the possibility or appearance of corruption in the electoral process. The objective is largely achieved through reasonable limitations on campaign contributions and through effective procedures for reporting and disclosure. Other objectives, though not unworthy, need to be balanced against the potential harm that they do the political process.

Those who testified before the Commission were almost unanimous in the view that current rules are too inflexible; that they require candidates to spend too much time collecting small contributions; that they may contribute inadvertently to increasing the length of the active phase of the campaign; that they reduce volunteer participation; and that they increase the possibility that national political action committees which make independent expenditures may have an unwarranted influence in future campaigns.

To alleviate these problems, the Commission (with the exception of Congressman Frenzel who differs on #1 below) makes the following recommendations:

1. Congress should increase the limit on an individual's campaign contribution in presidential nominating campaigns from $1000 to $5000. This figure should be adjusted automatically for every election year to take account of inflation.

2. Congress should abolish state-by-state limitations on campaign expenditures.

Conclusion

The nominating process is an intensely political event, involving the contest of vital issues, the play of competing interests, and the struggle for place among the nation's foremost political leaders. Changes in the formal provisions of the nominating system, no matter how well conceived, cannot guarantee satisfactory results. But a judicious set of rules and laws can avoid intensifying the difficulties inherent in the process and at the same time create decision making procedures that encourage the exercise of sound political judgment. No more—but no less—should be demanded of this process.

Conditions today are more favorable to a resolution of the nominating problem than at any other time in recent history. The nation's political leaders share an appreciation of the difficulties and a strong desire to resolve them. No political issue so divides the nation that institutional questions cannot be considered on their own merits. And finally, experience gained from the reforms of the past decade has made legislators and party leaders more aware of the limits and possibilities of institutional change. Now is the time for intelligent action, and we urge all those who can assist to join in the task of reform.